Television That Matters

Also by David L. Smith

Mass Media
Video Communication: Structuring Content For Maximum Program Effectiveness

Novels in the five-part series, *The Path Of The Jaguar* <www.Amazon.com>
Jaguar Rising: A Novel of the Ancient Maya
Jaguar Wind and Waves: A Novel of the Early Classic Maya

Fine Art Photography Series <www.blurb.com/bookstore>
Auto Reflections
Flowers
Milestones
Patterns
Reverence For Light
Wisdom Of The Spheres

Television That Matters

A Guide For Writers and Producers

DAVID L. SMITH

ISBN-13: 978-1463789589
ISBN-10: 1463789580

Cover photo and design by David L. Smith

Printed in the United States of America

Dedicated To

Barbara Marx Hubbard whose vision of both a positive future and expanded human capacities inspired the author's quest to understand and synthesize this vision of television's higher potentials.

Oprah Winfrey who, by modeling and championing personal transformation, demonstrated that the higher capacities of commercial television could be realized and made profitable for all stakeholders.

Acknowledgements

The author expresses deep appreciation to Michael Schwager and Barbara Marx Hubbard in particular, for the many conversations that contributed to the views expressed in both the text and the programming ideas in the Appendix.

Contents

Introduction

IN JULY OF 1980 I WAS IN WASHINGTON D.C. WAITING FOR A TAXI TO take me to the airport, returning from a weekend gathering of visionaries and space experts who were discussing the possibility of a "Mission to Haley's Comet." The idea was to launch a video camera that would dock with the comet and send back pictures that would be offered as a live, ticketed attraction in motion picture theaters around the world. I was a television producer at the time, working for a PBS station, there to interview the host of the gathering. I was not involved in the project.

Standing on the porch of the estate where the meeting was held, I struck up a conversation with an attendee whom I hadn't met. "So," he said, "what's television going to be like when it works?" I made a casual comment, my taxi came and that was the end of it. Actually, that was the beginning. What an odd question, I thought. How presumptuous.

Before wheels-down in Cincinnati I was pondering the gentleman's question but in a more positive and realistic light. Indeed, what *would* television be like if it worked, if it met the actual needs, wants, and interests of viewers? Long story short, that question sparked a decades-long quest to explore and envision television's higher potentials, it's capabilities beyond but including news, information, and entertainment. One of the conclusions I reached later on—and still hold—took the form of a paradox. On the one hand television needs a complete and extreme makeover. On the other hand, it's being and doing precisely what it needs to do in order to evolve.

On the negative side, as a mirror of society, commercial television presents a diluted, inaccurate, biased, and narrowly focused picture of life and living. Its predilection toward the sensational with a focus on violence, competition, sexuality, and other body functions is characteristic of adolescence. Accordingly, it glamorizes bad behavior, ignorance and base values while presenting erroneous and incomplete portrayals of what it means to be human. But if we stand back far enough and situate the industry within the broader context of social evolution, it becomes apparent that television is a work in progress, evolving in parallel with the predominant public consciousness—our interests, beliefs, preferences, values, and worldview. As a matter of supply and demand, the industry is simply providing what we want to watch. (More accurately, it's providing what *survey data* says the majority of viewers are watching). It must. Otherwise, it would not survive. So while television isn't all that it can be, it is on a growth trajectory.

The negative perspective urges us to do whatever we can to change the system: reduce that which diminishes, and introduce that which enriches. The more positive view suggests that things are fine as they are; leave the programming alone. So what's a responsible writer, producer, or citizen-viewer to do?

Responsible parents face the same dilemma regarding their children: they are already perfect in their *being*, yet they need substantial guidance and experience in the area of *becoming*. Left alone, children are not likely to develop the educational or social skills that contribute to a healthy, happy, contributing, and fulfilled adulthood. So the course taken here is the same that any responsible parent would take regarding their adolescent offspring: embrace the paradox by respecting the status quo while providing exposure to the advantages of maturity. So although these pages are not without criticism, our focus here will be on television's higher, largely untapped potentials in both these areas.

Like it or not, experience it or not, change is happening. Continuously. As with human beings, the transition from adolescence to adulthood can, when approached with caring, understanding, and an eye toward the benefits of maturity, be graceful.

The perspectives and guidance offered here is directed mainly to students and industry professionals who want their works to make a positive difference in the lives of viewers, television managers and creative people who are looking for a higher level of personal satisfaction, writers and producers who want their programs to be both substantive and entertaining, providers who want to respond to the *authentic* and *higher* needs, wants, interests, and aspirations of the public —as well as meet the needs of commerce.

Because the components of this vision are based upon an emerging social paradigm and whole-systems science, these are elaborated after a brief discussion of the personal and social significance of television. Following this, the metaphor of television as a social nervous system and the governing values that derive from it, lead to descriptions and examples of programming that matters.

Because the public will not watch programs that are didactic, dry, or boring, concept development processes and guidelines are provided to show how mindful, substantive programming can—and must—be entertaining and/or compelling.

The final sections of the book specify what viewers can do to gracefully nudge the industry toward maturity. Industry professionals and students aspiring to enter the field will find guidance and practical information on how to get started on the path toward creating real value programming.

To help clarify the definition of television that matters in the area of programming, the Appendix provides examples of original programming concepts taken from the author's collection. It is hoped that they will inspire readers to generate, develop, and produce their own ideas.

Part I

The Significance Of Television

1

Television Already Matters

Television appears to have a greater influence on the structure of daily life than any other innovation in this century.

John Condry

DURING THE COURSE OF A VIGOROUS PANEL DISCUSSION ABOUT television influence, one of the participants grew weary of the barrage of negative consequences attributed to heavy television viewing. "Gimme a break," the producer said. "We're talkin' about television here!" His exasperation was sparked by the other panelists criticizing the medium for presenting content that's simplistic, narrow-minded, trivial, and in many instances erroneous, fueling an already overly materialistic society. "Folks," he said. "Aside from the news, it's entertainment! Nobody takes this stuff seriously. The public sees through the glamour and sales pitches. They know it's all edited and staged. Of course, kids are sucked into it if they watch too much of it. But most adults know better. I grew up watching a lot of television. I watch a lot of it now. My family and I don't have any of the problems the others are talking about. Neither do my neighbors. And hey, if you don't like it turn it off. Nobody's forcing you to watch."

That's a valid perspective. Trouble is, we're not turning it off. And research shows that television is a major contributor to socialization in America. It's not only shaping the culture, it's defining our personal realities. Like it or not. Admit it or not. Television exerts a profound influence on viewers and non-viewers alike, irrespective of age, ethnicity, education, socio-economic status or position.

Duane Elgin (Social visionary):

> "Television is not just another technology. It's at the very heart of our capacity for self-reflective consciousness at a societal scale. It's our social witness, our vehicle for knowing what we know as nations and as a human family. Television has become the social brain or central nervous system of the human family" (Elgin, 1993).

Television and related technologies that provide programming such as radio, motion pictures, and the internet are *media* in the truest sense of the word. Well beyond being devices that provide information and entertainment, they are *environments* within which we construct our personal and social realities, environments that contribute to our definition of what it means to be human. As such it's appropriate to say that we not only experience the electronic media, we live within them. And we don't have to own a TV set or watch television to be influenced by it.

Narain Dass Batra (Political scientist):

> "In terms of helping us understand the world we live in, our television environment is as important a part of our environment as air and water are in our physical environment" (Batra, 1990).

The late governor of Florida, LeRoy Collins, considered television to be "the greatest single power in the hands of mortal man."

E.B. White (American essayist):

> "We shall stand or fall by television, of that I am sure. I believe television is going to be the test of the modern world, and that in this new opportunity to see beyond the range of our vision we shall discover either a new and unbearable disturbance of the general peace, or a saving radiance in the sky. That radiance falls unevenly today. It is still a dim light in education. It has not fulfilled its potential for children. It has neglected the needs of public television. And in the electoral process it has cast a dark shadow."

Like the producer on the panel referred to earlier said, if we don't like television we don't have to watch. Consciously or not, each of us decides the place of television and the other electronic media in our lives, and the lives of our children. Like any tool, it's wise to use it with caution and some honest self-awareness. For instance, asking: Am I better for watching this? Or better off without it?

WHAT GIVES TELEVISION ITS POWER?

Memes

British scientist Richard Dawkins coined the word "meme" to explain the spread of ideas and cultural phenomena such as melodies, catch phrases, jargon, buzzwords, fashion, labels, and other social icons (Dawkins, 1976). These "units of culture" are transmitted from one mind to another with the effect that each repetition contributes to its standing within the cultural reality. Memes are contagious and they build on one another.

Television and the other electronic media, sometimes purposefully, more often not, are constantly injecting memes into the social body. The names of celebrities, logos, and brand names are all memes. Advertisers especially have learned that we don't simply purchase products because of their attributes or associated benefits, we also want the identifications, lifestyles, or perceptions that connect us to the culture. Acceptance. Status. Membership in the "cool" club. Memes can deliver because they provide the labels, the sounds, and the look. When it comes to creating and introducing memes into the culture, no other medium comes even close to matching television's effectiveness.

Stimulation

The human brain, nervous system, and senses are wired to involuntarily attend to "strange things, moving things, wild animals, bright things, pretty things, metallic things, words, blows, and blood" (James, 1985). Especially things that change. Our senses evolved and became integrated capacities because they had survival value.

Relevant to our consideration of the power of television is the fact that the eyes, contrary to popular belief, do not see. Their function is to collect light impulses, data for the *brain* to interpret into information, images, and ultimately meaning. The eyes detect this data through differences in changing movements, colors, textures, patterns, edge effects and rhythms. It's only when this data is transmitted to the brain and combined with past experience that we perceive and distinguish, the difference between a pencil and a pencil fish. The clue for writers and producers who want to provide stimulation to attract and hold their viewer's attention, is that human beings (and some of our pets) are attracted to the television screen simply because it changes. A key contributor to television's power is the fact that stimulation of the senses is biologically positive.

Immediacy

What we see on television appears to be happening now, live, even when we know we're looking at a recording or replay. The look and feel of the pictures combined with sound contributes to the impression that what's on the screen is actually happening in the present. And if the presentation is interesting, dramatic, or exciting, it engages us. We want to be "in on it." At the very least, we want to know about it. As social creatures we're naturally curious about life and how it's being experienced by other people. And it gives us something to talk about, another point of connection and dimension. This too, is biologically positive because it has survival value. The illusion of immediacy is powerful because it puts us in touch with the world and our times. We feel we're a part of it, if only as observers.

Reach

Television is a *mass* medium, now having the potential to be received by every individual on the planet. Because television signals have no boundaries, memes can and do cross borders. Easily. The tearing down of the Berlin Wall and the revolution for democracy in Egypt are just two examples of what happens on a large scale when an oppressed people see on television how they are being deprived and how other people are living more free, comfortable, and enjoyable lifestyles. Again, curiosity: we want to see, know, and experience what everyone else is seeing, knowing, and experiencing. Television is powerful in this regard, not only because it can reach a global audience, but also, by providing models it extends the range of human capability: what we can do individually and collectively.

Novelty

The desire for novelty, to experience the unusual and new, is a characteristic of all living systems. Because it stimulates reflection and creates options, novelty is necessary for human survival and development. It's the reason why we're compelled to watch people on the screen behaving badly, saying stupid things, or making sensational displays: the *difference* between "normal" and unusual—foreground to background, hot to cold, good guy versus bad guy—generates information. As we shall see, information provides advantages for survival and growth. Often through humor, novelty on television shows us there are other ways of being and more perceptions of what is real than the one we experience.

Shared Experience

Because potentially millions of people are watching what we're watching and at the same time, the subconscious mind makes the assumption that what we are seeing is both *real* and *normal*. Whatever the event, theme, or experience, the unspoken and underlying assumption is that we are seeing *how* life is, *what* people are like, and *how* the world works. Television shows us who we are as a people: what we care about, how we see the world, what we value, how we relate to others and the environment, and how we respond to change.

In observing this, we are changed and unwittingly become agents of change to a lesser or greater extent. Witness the mentality of the terrorist and that of the monk. Both can walk through the same crowd and each will have a dramatically different experience of it. While shared experiences can generate feelings of connection and momentum, the propensity to "see what we want to see" and "find what we look for" validates our perception about these things, whatever the experience might be. Apart from marketing issues, this is one of the main reasons why writers and producers are advised to know their audience.

Empathy

Television engages our natural inclination to enter into the emotional experiences of others. Screen characters and presenters provide opportunities for us to share their ups and downs, trials, tribulations, successes, and failures by identifying with them in consciousness rather than physically. Once the television screen attracts our attention, empathy is the magnet that pulls us into the experiences of the people we find there.

Multiple Realities

How other people live, their values, lifestyles, perceptions, values, the manner of their speaking and dress are all intrinsically interesting. It's not just that we're fascinated by differences in personal expression, these differences validate and help us shape our own perceptions and expressions. Every program, commercial, movie, or promotional message represents the *consciousness* of the writers and producers. To experience the product of their creative choices is to live for a time in their realities, even in works of fiction. Seeing how other people live, work, and make decisions is compelling because we're seeking confirmation of our own ways as part of an ongoing process to construct a personal reality that's as comfortable, enjoyable, profitable, meaningful, and satisfying as we can make it.

ALL TELEVISION VIEWING HAS CONSEQUENCES

Did you notice a pattern in the above forces that give television its power? Indeed, they command our attention and influence our lives, especially at the subconscious level, because they emerged from the deep evolutionary past when they were necessary for survival and growth. In large part they contributed to our biological and emotional inheritance. And that's why television, which combines, amplifies, and extends them, has the power to shape our individual and collective realities, sometimes before we can even walk. As Joshua Meyrowitz puts it, "Television takes our kids across the globe before parents give them permission to cross the street."

While the act of watching television doesn't appear to produce noticeable effects in us, it nonetheless has profound effects on the subconscious mind. Television experiences not only convey *memes* that operate below the level of conscious awareness, they feed the brain-nervous system stimuli that are used to interpret the world and construct meaning. "At a higher level they illuminate and interpret the human condition, influence decision-making, stimulate the molecules of emotion, help us construct our identity, and perceive the world" (Pert, 1999). Television indoctrinates and educates. Former chairman of the Federal Communications Commission, (FCC) Nicholas Johnson, encapsulated the significance when he said, "All of television is educational. The only question is: What does it teach?"

Before we move into considerations of what television could or should be teaching, a reality-check is in order regarding the status quo. As noted in the introduction, television has both positive and negative affects.

Negative Effects

The following are just a few of the many conclusions drawn from research studies on television effects. Aside from showing that there's a downside to overindulging in television, the list should help parents err on the side of caution. Web sites on these issues are abundantly available on the internet.

Television can—

- Negatively affect the developing brain (myelination*, memory, attention, focus).
- Displace direct personal experience.
- Significantly influence attitudes, body image, perceptions of self and others.
- Normalize aggression, violence, self-centeredness, materialism, and greed.
- Generate, validate, and maintain stereotypes.
- Have a desensitizing and habituating effect; increased exposure reduces sensitivity.
- Induce passivity and inhibit creative activity.
- Invite imitation, notably in the areas of violence, crime, aggressive behavior, and suicide.
- Encourage cynicism, skepticism, and a lack of trust in others.
- Contribute to a negative view of life and living, the "mean-world syndrome."

* Heavy viewing has been shown to retard the *mylination* process in the early brain (Pearce, 1992). Myelination is the process whereby nerve cells in the brain build up a fatty protein sheath that improves conductivity, enhancing the flow of information from one cell to another. If this process is retarded, there's a loss in the ability to use the imagination and to generate personal fantasies and realities from within (Buzzell, 1998).

Positive Effects

Television can—

- Educate. ("Sesame Street," "NOVA," historical dramas, cooking, etc.).
- Relax and distract.
- Present points of view different from our own.
- Entertain, provide welcome variety and diversions from everyday stresses.
- Provide information and access to the happenings of the day.
- Inform and warn about changing climate conditions and national disasters.
- Provide access to and information about special interests.
- Inspire and improve creative skills.
- Provides vicarious and empathetic experience.

Part II

Whole Systems Theory

2

A Whole-Systems Primer

A human being is part of the Whole... He experiences himself, his thoughts and feelings, as something separated from the rest... a kind of optical delusion of his consciousness. This delusion is a kind of prison for us, restricting us to our personal desires and to affection for a few persons nearest us. Our task must be to free ourselves from this prison by widening our circle of compassion to embrace all living creatures and the whole of nature in its beauty. Nobody is able to achieve this completely, but the striving for such achievement is, in itself, a part of the liberation and a foundation for inner security.

Albert Einstein

THE PATTERNS OBSERVED IN NATURE WERE DISCUSSED AND documented in China as early as five thousand years ago. They were again articulated poetically by Lao Tzu (Gia-fu, 1972) in the 6th Century B.C. In the modern era, Ludwig von Bertalanffy examined these pattern and developed principles based on part-whole relationships, which came to the attention of engineers and physical scientists with the publication of his book on general systems theory (Bertalanffy, 1968). Because it became a useful tool in the physical sciences, the theory developed into the field known today as General Systems Science.

A decade after Bertalanffy introduced his theories or mechanism, James Grier Miller elaborated them and applied them to *living* entities in his seminal work entitled, *Living Systems* (Miller, 1978). Since then, scholars, scientists, engineers, information theorists, artists, and philosophers have drawn on these sources and created a gestalt, a way of thinking about both mechanical and living systems—from cell to wristwatch to universe—in order to better understand, appreciate, and manage complexity. (The story is told that after President Kennedy committed the nation to the moon mission, NASA scientists drew heavily upon general systems science to insure a successful outcome.)

Systems thinking is essentially an organized way of seeing and gaining insight by understanding part-whole relationships and their functionality. It has enjoyed long-term and widespread application in both mechanical and human systems including the development of human capital, team building, nurturing synergy, project development, organizational development, and business management to name a few. The application here is especially appropriate because commercial television networks, channels, and stations are both businesses and complex living systems consisting of hierarchies of people in functional relationship.

System

According to Bertalanffy, "A system can be defined as a set of elements standing in interrelations." There are two major classifications: mechanical and living. Mechanical systems perform a function according to a design. The cars coming off assembly lines began as mental images and then designs on paper or computer before they could become functioning vehicles. Living systems on the other hand, have an implied function that derives from their livingness, their inherent vitality. They want to stay alive and grow and evolve to higher orders of complexity and awareness. Within both systems scientists discriminate between "simple" systems that have few parts, and "complex" systems that have many parts. The more parts there are in an assemblage, the more complex the relations between them. And the more complex the relations, the more vulnerable the whole becomes to breakdown, and therefore the greater the need for attention—maintenance and management—in order to overcome every system's worst nightmare. Entropy.

Entropy

The term *entropy* relates to the Second Law of Thermodynamics which states that matter dissipates. In time, all matter breaks down. Atoms eventually diffuse and revert back to heat energy. Matter is in a constant state of disintegration. Metals rusts. Computers fail. From a *living* systems perspective, this means that everything dies. Bodies grow old and die. Noise disrupts communication. Relationships and businesses fail. Nations and civilizations come to an end.

If it comes as bad news that all systems are moving inexorably toward breakdown and dissipation, the good news is that it can be delayed. For instance, health promoting acts can keep the human body functioning longer. And maintaining equipment will have the same affect. The systems term for acts that retard entropy is "negative entropy," or neg-entropy. In the social sciences the preferred term is *syntropy*.

Syntropy

Any action or force that puts off or retards entropy is considered syntropic. Oiling a metallic surface prevents it from rusting. Putting fresh batteries in an electronic device keeps it running. Good dental hygiene prevents gum disease and promotes heart health. Feeding, complementing, and rewarding a work crew encourages better performance. Frequent communication improves relationships. So whenever a breakdown occurs, the appropriate response is to view the dysfunction as the work of entropy and initiate acts of syntropy. Qualities and acts that are especially syntropic include:

Inputting Information. The more information and the better its quality, the greater the reduction of entropy. Without the information shared back and forth between Apollo 13 and her ground crews, the astronauts would not have survived.

Creating Order. In itself, order and acts of ordering within living systems contribute to maintenance and survival because they keeping the parts in right functional relationship. We may need a microscope or telescope to see the order in the micro and macro worlds, but throughout there is astonishing order. The more a system is organized the greater it resilience in the wake of entropy.

Increased Communication. More and better communication promotes knowledge, understanding, and the desire to do what's necessary to keep a system functioning.

Creating A Positive Field. Comfortable physical and emotional climates promote enjoyment and right relationship which, in turn promotes increased cooperation and collaboration.

Holon

A holon is another word for whole-system. While it refers to an individual system such as a person, it carries with it the characteristic of interdependence. So the term "holon" is used to include the larger context of relatedness and interdependence, to signal that the system in question is composed of lower order systems—sub-systems—and at the same time has membership in higher order systems. All living systems, by virtue of their structure and considered as a unit, are holons. For instance, the human body is a holon. It's constituted of lower-order, less complex holons. In descending order these are organs, cells, molecules, atoms, and sub-atomic energy fields. At the same time, the human body has membership in higher order holons. In roughly ascending order these are family, church, business, community, nation, and species. One of the defining features of *living*, as opposed to *mechanical*, systems is that they are in the middle, constituted of lower order holons and members of higher order holons. Lower order holons are not inferior. They are just less complex than higher order holons. Without them, the higher order holons would not exist.

Synergy

(Not to be confused with *syntropy*). Systems are said to be *synergistic* when the output or outcome of the whole is greater than the sum of its parts. The child is neither a copy of the father nor the mother, but a totally unique individual unto himself. Socially, acts of creative collaboration, genuine caring, sharing, and empowering creates a vitality that strengthens and unifies the whole corporation or community. When people see themselves as contributors working collaboratively toward a meaningful goal which they had a hand in determining, they take more ownership of it, identify with it and invest more time, energy and creativity in realizing it.

Synergy becomes possible when the members of a team are so in love with a vision, they become dedicated as a matter of personal choice to realizing it. Love makes us capable of transcending individual, even collective strivings. When a team comes together like that, one plus one equals four. It's commonplace to see this operating in sports and music, even in the military where life and death situations can create powerful bonds.

Unfortunately, the business world with its penchant for buzzwords adopted the term "synergy" in the eighties to characterize high-performance teams. These processes, including "six-sigma," strive for zero defects within a system. While that's admirable and good, the outcome is still one plus one equals two.

Rigorously speaking, synergy isn't about high-performance. It's about *transcendence*, overcoming limits and limited thinking, bonding, and attainment beyond expectation. Having personally experienced it, the author can attest that one plus one can equal four.

Synergy is both rare and rarifying. Even when outsiders observe the team in action, they feel electricity in the air. Members can't wait to get out of bed in the morning to be with their colleagues. When functioning together they're in the flow. Time stands still. Peak experiences and feelings of love become frequent. These and other positive and empowering feelings are an indication of true synergy. Can it be forced? No. Can it be nurtured? Definitely. (See Chapter 16).

Feedback

A system is maintained within specified limits by providing information about how well or how poorly it's performing relative to its purpose. Since systems exist for a reason, it's important to know whether or not, how well or how poorly, that reason is being actualized. And that's where feedback comes in.

There are two forms: positive and negative. Both are important. And the more feedback, the better. When a stand-up comedian gets a laugh, she knows that her delivery was effective. That's positive feedback. If she repeats that performance, she is likely to get a similar outcome. On the other hand, if she doesn't get a laugh where she expects it, the negative feedback tells her something didn't work. If she's determined to use the material that got a negative response, then she needs to revise either the material or her presentation. Without the benefit of feedback—audience reaction—she would have no way of knowing whether or not her performance was successful.

Feedback is syntropic because it generates *information* that produces *learning*. The more feedback, the better the learning. And the better the quality of the feedback, the better the quality of learning. For instance in the 1950s, door-to-door interviews about television viewing patterns were conducted to measure audience size, but they did a poor job of providing networks with quality information. Studies showed that people often reported watching programs that they *valued*, rather than the ones they actually *watched*. Others gave responses intended to impress the interviewers. Poor sampling information yields poor learning. Within both mechanical and living systems, feedback can be used to enhance future operational effectiveness.

WHOLE-SYSTEM PRINCIPLES

The research relating to systems science referred to at the beginning of the chapter are thick books filled with technical jargon. For the sake of brevity and clarity, some of key principles that relate to effectively managing complex social systems—such as television stations and production companies—have been condensed below.

The Weakest Link

A system is as strong as its weakest link. The link that breaks when a chain is put under stress is the *part* within the whole system that becomes dysfunctional soonest. To counteract the weak link principle, managers hire the strongest employees possible. Human Resource professionals get the best information they can. Technicians maintain or replace equipment that is faltering. And individuals seeking careers invest time, money, and energy in building character and competencies.

Equifinality

The Principle of Equifinality says that each and every part of a system has equal opportunity to affect the outcome of the system—its purpose or function. If and when we change any *part* of a mechanical system or *member* of a living system, the operation or outcome is affected. The system performs differently than it otherwise would. No matter how small or seemingly insignificant the part or member, each exerts an influence on the system's performance. An orchestra or rock group performs differently every time they take the stage. Things happen. One musician substitutes for another. A different saxophone mouthpiece generates a different sound. The drummer misses a beat. A depressed singer doesn't deliver his usual energy.

Likewise, corporate cultures change when employees begin eating lunch at their desks or when people wear jeans to work. It's the reason we can't step into the same river twice. It's not the same stream it was even a second ago because the elements—water, stones, leaves, air currents, pollution—have changed. Each and every part or member within a system, no matter how insignificant seeming, has equal opportunity to—and does—affect its performance or outcome. The production of a television interview considered as a whole system, is different when even a microphone is changed or shown in the shot. Change one word in a drama script and it's a different story.

The Whole Organizes The Parts / Members

Since *purpose* is the reason for a systems existence, every part or member of the system derives its identity and function from that purpose. In order for the whole to function in ways that assure the realization of its purpose, decisions relating to the parts or members must refer to the purpose because the whole specifies and organizes the parts according to its design.

A wristwatch keeps time because the parts have been specified and organized according to a design that meets this purpose. If members of a television crew organize themselves according to the needs of the director and follow the script, the result will be the accomplishment of their common purpose, a program. Consider the human being. The whole person, not just the brain, regulates our cells and organs. Rigorously speaking, it's the purpose of the whole person (which usually operates sub-consciously) that determines, coordinates, and regulates the component organs. We don't have to tell the lower-level holons such as the eyes, feet, and hands what to do. They perform automatically by virtue of they're being organized by the whole. The more we become aware of our purpose in life the better we can organize the physical members and our mental, emotional, and spiritual capacities, to accomplish it.

The Key To Managing Complexity Is To Manage The Parts Or Members

This principle is the key to the efficient and effective management of complex systems. If we consistently attend to the *integrity* and *interactions* of the *parts* in mechanical systems and *members* in living systems, the performance or outcome is assured. Apart from outside or unforeseen influences, the system's purpose is likely to be realized.

When a television script contains deep emotion or fascinating experiences, when the director, performers, and members of the production crew are performing at peak, and when their functional relationships compliment each other, the resulting program is likely to succeed. Whatever the goal—creating a work of art, launching a space taxi, building a synergistic team, starting a small business, raising happy, healthy, and contributing children—success is in the details, attending to the parts or members to insure their individual integrity and effective functioning. It's this principle that generated the adage: "God is in the details." The most efficient and effective way to arrive at a successful outcome in social systems is to pay attention to the individual members, and to organize things so each of them, at their level, pay attention to their functional details.

When systems break down or fail, the appropriate fix or solution is to focus on the individual parts. It's the message of *Zen And The Art Of Motorcycle Maintenance*. When your motorcycle fails to start, kicking the tires and swearing at the bike will never make it start. What's needed is a calm assessment of each part, beginning with the most obvious: Have I run out of gas? Did the ignition cable break or disconnect? (Persig, 1974).

Life had to build functioning, self-sustaining, and self-making cells before they could combine into a functional organism. And so on up the levels of complexity to societies and nations. To repair or heal living systems, begin at the lowest level possible.

Part III

Paradigms

3

The Phenomenon Of Paradigms

If ten people walk beyond civilization and build a new sort of life for themselves, then those ten people are already living in the next paradigm, from the first day.

Daniel Quinn

IN THE MID-TO-LATE 50'S ADVERTISERS SHIFTED AWAY FROM promoting a product's tangible attributes, appealing instead to the desire for its associated status and lifestyle benefits, particularly in the areas of appearance, sex, wealth, power, glamour, and excitement. The strategy of drawing an association between a product or service and images of happiness and glamour was so successful on television it's still the gold standard for selling the American dream—one toothpaste, one automobile, and now one prescription drug at a time. The television and advertising industries have become so skilled at using memes to accomplish this, viewers don't realize that the preponderance of commercial television programming including news, entertainment, and talk formats involves some form of selling or promotion. By definition (and contrary to the public's wish that it be otherwise) commercial television is largely about commerce.

Into the 60's and beyond, the underlying and cumulative message of television advertising was that the pursuit of happiness was realized through the acquisition of the newest, most affordable, best, most beautiful, helpful, useful, life enhancing, freedom-promoting products and services, especially those that helped us become more acceptable in the areas of relationship, fame, and fortune. "Relieve pain fast." "Stop underarm odor." "We're worth it." Save money. Don't wait. But what's a woman to do once she has her dream lover, the wedding, car, house, washer and dryer, 3D television set, iPhone and iPad, steady income, and 2.5 kids?

At some point in life questions arise concerning authenticity. Discounting other people's expectations or impressions, we ask questions of meaning: What do I really want? Who am I? What is the true me? Why am I doing this? And then we address the questions of value: What's really important? What would make me happy? What really matters? How should I spend my time? *Having* and *doing* cannot guarantee satisfaction or lasting happiness. While possessions and experiences may contribute to our comfort and enjoyment, they are usually short lived. Lasting joy, satisfaction, and fulfillment come from states of *being* that derive from gaining clarity about our true and unique identity, place, purpose, and mission.

Whether we look for answers from traditional sources outside ourselves or from self examination or a combination of both, our perception of the world and our place in it is largely determined by our answers to these, "perennial," questions. And others: How did we get here? Why are we here? How can we make the best of it? In every era notable thinkers develop speculations and theories in response to these questions, and their cultures adopt them as world-views—paradigms—that explain the nature of "reality." As perceptions change, for instance as a result of more experience and increased knowledge, paradigms change.

SCIENTIFIC MATERIALISM
THE PARADIGM OF SEPARATION AND FEAR

The Copernican Revolution ushered in a paradigm shift in the 16th century when Nicolaus Copernicus discovered that, contrary to the preceding Ptolemaic paradigm that viewed the Earth as the center of the universe, our planet is one among many that orbit the Sun. This shift in perception brought about the Scientific Revolution and along with it the notion that science is the *only* route to true knowledge, and that matter alone is the proper domain of science because it can be sensed and verified through repeated experience.

The next great shift reinforced these perceptions. Toward the beginning of the 18th century, Sir Isaac Newton laid the groundwork for most of classical and celestial mechanics—physics—by describing gravity and showing that the motion of objects both on Earth and in the heavens are governed by the same set of natural laws. His conclusion was that the Earth and all heavenly bodies operate like a precision machine—a clock. Today it would be the computer. Newtonian physics introduced perceptions that, while erroneous, are still being taught in high schools and colleges today: that matter is composed of irreducible and discrete atoms, that matter is primal, the basic stuff of the universe, that as parts in a gigantic cosmic machine all the elements of the universe, including people, are separate and autonomous, and all conform to the same set of universal laws of gravity and motion.

In 1859 Charles Darwin helped establish the theory of evolution. While the theory holds up in important ways, the mechanisms he postulated to explain its workings have been disproved over and again. Darwin is nonetheless given credit for introducing the paradigm of Scientific Materialism, the idea that life on this planet is an accident of random mutation, and that it's the fittest who survive because they live to reproduce.

The pursuit of knowledge in the past was predicated upon the truth or falsity of a set of perceptions. But when we look at the various crises facing individuals, nations and the planet today, many leading thinkers are denying that there is an objective truth that can be known, given enough time. Their approach is instead to ask about the *consequences* of perception itself. What for instance was the consequence of the perception that Germany was the master race? Since perception determines individual behavior and we tend to create what we perceive, what perceptions would motivate and guide us to build the kind of world we want, a world that works for everyone?

Even a cursory glance at consequences indicates that scientific materialism is not working. The belief that *matter* is primal has led to the inordinate consumerism that's overtaxing the global environment. The idea that human beings are dispensable cogs in a machine is depressing and disempowering. The illusion that we are separate promotes adversarial relations and diminishes our innate propensities for empathy and compassion. The notion that it's the fittest who survive is the law of the jungle—eat or be eaten. Competition is so engrained in the fabric of the American culture, producers have a hard time even conceiving of a "reality" program that doesn't have winners and losers.

The bumper-sticker adage that says, "He who dies with the most toys wins," is the sentiment par excellence of the independence paradigm, which in clinical terms, amounts to an autoimmune disorder. Human beings, the cells of the global body, are disadvantaging each other. Nevertheless, over time we learn. Engineer and systems innovator Buckminster Fuller said, "You can't learn less. You can only learn more." What this means is that breakdowns are providing the feedback humanity needs in order to create more viable perceptions, those that result in realities that have positive, life enhancing consequences for all.

"EMERGENTS" LEAD THE TRANSITION

Working without the constraints of bureaucratic structures and social norms, caring and creative people begin thinking in new ways, valuing what is not traditionally valued, undertaking positive change initiatives irrespective of time, money, or resources. Technically referred to as "emergents," these people choose to live the changes they want to see in the world. Their life and work-styles are motivated by an understanding of their personal purpose coupled with a desire to live and contribute in ways that are meaningful, less stressful, and fulfilling. They choose to work in the flow of what gives them joy, and they find it in authentic living and paving the way to a better world for all.

According to Joel Barker if we want to find out where the new paradigm will show up, the place to look is wherever people are saying, "No way. It can't be done." "That won't work." "It'll never sell!" (Barker, 1989). To the contrary, human flight, the telephone and electric light bulb, the four-minute mile (all sports records for that matter), delivering men home safely from the moon, life extension, artificial organs and transplants, bionics, gene splicing, the personal computer, iPods, e-readers, and the internet are just some of the more obvious examples of inventions and innovations we didn't know we needed and now can't live without. Advances in technology are widely reported, but those in science and especially social engineering have been underrepresented in the media.

In both mechanical and social systems, crisis precedes transformation. Mechanical breakdowns call for a response to fix the problem, improve the system or replace it. In social systems, individual(s) dissatisfied with the way things are—emergents—see a better way and take it upon themselves to create change, if only in themselves or their immediate group. So although breakdowns in the existing order of social systems are undesirable and at times painful, they can call forth responses that often lead to new thinking and seeing.

Conventional television structures, operations, and offerings emerged in an era of secular scientific materialism when competition and consumerism were paramount. That wasn't bad. It was necessary. But in a world where those values are increasingly undermining and threatening the safety, health, and well-being of people and animals, where the world's natural resources are being over exploited and environments threatened, the perception that we are separate and responsible only to and for ourselves—individually and nationally—is becoming toxic. And because it poses a survival threat, the breakdowns we've been experiencing in every sphere of human activity are calling for more viable perceptions of life and living.

INTERDEPENDENCE
THE PARADIGM OF UNITY AND LOVE

For a set of ideas to constitute a true paradigm shift, if they're to overturn previous perceptions and have traction in everyday life, they must pass muster on the street and be grounded in science. Especially, the behaviors that result from the practices they espouse must deliver improved and sustainable conditions for all. And on a global scale. The paradigm of interdependence that provides the foundation for this vision of television's higher potentials, not only meets these criteria, it derives from them.

The view that all living things constitute one, interconnected and interdependent whole, regards matter and spirit as two sides of the same coin. The more we learn about the physical world, the more we come to discern and appreciate the mysteries of life and the cosmos. And the more we delve into the mysteries of consciousness and spirit, the more effective we become as individuals and co-creators of the physical world. As complimentary ways of knowing and relating to the full spectrum of life, both these areas deserve serious attention and respect. And they are getting it. The Institute of Noetic Sciences is a research organization that has successfully integrated the internal and external domains of human experience. Their stated purpose (<*www.noetic.org*>) is, "To help birth a new *worldview* that recognizes our basic interconnectedness and interdependence and promotes the flourishing of life in all its magnificent forms."

After thirteen years of research, sociologist Paul Ray and psychologist Sherry Ruth Anderson identified fifty million "cultural creatives," Americans who "care deeply about ecology and saving the planet, about relationships, peace, and social justice, about self-actualization, spirituality, and self-expression" (Ray, 2000). And after conducting hundreds of interviews with people who identified with the paradigm of interdependence, Arjuna Ardagh identified a global trend, which he calls: *The Translucent Revolution* (Ardagh, 2005).

TENANTS OF THE NEW PARADIGM

While this following perceptions relating to the paradigm of interdependence are incomplete and merely a sketch of concepts that would require volumes to describe adequately, they're presented here to provide an overview of the shift from separation and fear to unity and love. If this sounds too sweet, idealistic. or impractical, it may be due to the culture not yet fully appreciating the power of the feminine—the art and practice of love and nurturing.

Unity Of All Life

The universe is one, a whole, living, creative, evolving, self-organizing, and self-making entity. The galaxies, stars and star-systems are holons, cells within the universal body. Likewise, human beings are holons, thinking cells that, along with the other life forms, constitute the life of the planetary body.

Energy

The laws of quantum physics indicate that the universe is constituted of energy. Energy is primal. Matter is derivative. There's far more information and potential in what we cannot see, than in what we do see.

Life

Life came from the stars, evolved, and is sustained on the planet by the Sun. (Native Americans pay tribute to Father Sky for creating life, and Mother Earth for sustaining it). Life proliferated and advanced through a process of adaptive mutation.

Life Processes

Enduring patterns in the evolutionary process demonstrate that life moves inexorably in the direction of increased freedom, order, diversity, novelty, complexity, and consciousness.

Evolution
Living systems, holons at every level, discover what works through breakdowns and crises. Evolution is not a random process. We are not here by accident. From the beginning, pattern, order, and increasing complexity are evident at every level of existence.

Inner / Outer
The inner world precipitates the outer world. Perceptions, beliefs, and attitudes trump genetic endowment. Through perception and belief we can modify 30,000 variations of every gene.

Purpose
The essence of who we are enters into life experience in order to learn, grow, expand, and evolve in consciousness.

Interdependence
Up and down the web of life, at every level, separation in the sense of independent entities living in isolation is an illusion. All living systems are interconnected and interdependent. Individual cells, organs, and human beings cannot survive for very long on their own. The same is true of living ecosystems such as companies, industries, institutions, and nations.

Competition and Cooperation
Evolutionary biologist Elisabet Sahtouris (Sahtouris, 2000) says, "Evolution depends on competition *and* cooperation, on independence *and* interdependence. Competition and independence are both important to individual survival, while cooperation and interdependence are both important to group, social, or species survival. Individuals and their society are holons at two levels of the same holarchy. These levels must achieve mutual consistency by looking out for themselves and working out between themselves a balance of competition and cooperation, of dependence and interdependence."

Holism
Holons are apparent at every level of being. Balance consists in maintaining and vitalizing them at every level so that, as we make our choices, the entities above and below are supported and sustained.

Ethics and Integrity

Having a moral-ethical framework insures that in challenging situations one's choices and behaviors do no harm to the whole, ideally contribute to its well-being. Integrity in this regard means being true to *higher* values. Adolph Hitler was a man of integrity. He had integrity to his dream of a master race. *What* we are true *to* is as important as being true to it.

Balance

Whole-systems balance requires harmonizing the components, all stakeholders. Harmony occurs more often when there is balance between matter and spirit, and heart and head.

Responsibility

As members of one, whole, and living body—the Earth—we are responsible for our actions with regard to it. Acting responsibly means responsible stewardship, doing no harm and preserving, ideally promoting, the health and well-being of the holons above and below us.

Authenticity

To live authentically is to make choices based upon the deepest part of our being—rather than the opinions or expectations of others. Or society.

4

The Shift In Business

The ultimate purpose of business is not, or should not be, simply to make money. Nor is it merely a system of making and selling things. The promise of business is to increase the general well being of humankind through service, a creative invention and ethical philosophy.

Paul Hawken

HOW DO THE TENANTS OF THE INTERDEPENDENCE PARADIGM relate to the world of business? Even a cursory search on the internet under the heading, "socially responsible business," or "corporate transformation" turns up hundreds of documents citing the national and multi-national corporations and small businesses that have aligned with it. Their entry point in many instances was largely due to the realization of their impact on the environment, a factor largely ignored by the television industry where the impact is mainly psychological and social.

Because the transformation requires shifts in *thinking* and *valuing*, it's important for us to get very specific about the nature of these shifts and consider the benefits they might bring to a more mature television enterprise. In practice, the substantive issues presented here are those that would need to be addressed, all of which would promote long term survival and enhance profitability. For those who remain skeptical, a little research into specific companies that identify themselves as "socially responsible" would show that these shifts in thinking are precisely those that contributed to their renewed vitality.

IDENTITY

Who are we as a business? What business are we in?

From: *We're in the information and entertainment business.*
To: *We're in the communication and human development business. Information and entertainment are the means to higher ends.*

Benefits this shift would bring—

- Through a shift in identity, the company would gain increased opportunity to diversify and expand.
- Viewers would become more responsible for their own, and their family's viewing choices because they would see themselves as members of larger, social and global, bodies.
- If media professionals saw themselves as interconnected and interdependent members of larger social systems, they would tend to work more responsibly. They would realize that their decisions impact the health and well-being of their viewers, society, the environment and themselves.
- A broader definition of corporate identity provides significantly increased opportunity for brand identification—an especially challenging area for television.
- Programs produced in the context of broader perspectives would show an immediate positive effect in the community.
- Viewers would appreciate and applaud the revised role of television in their lives and in the life of the community.

OWNERSHIP

Who owns this business? Who are the caretakers?

From: *Owners and shareholders own the company.*
To: *We are owned by a community of stakeholders.*

The true owners of a business are those who, by virtue of having a stake in the enterprise, assume responsibility for its health, well-being, and growth. Whatever the role, all stakeholders have a right to participate in the decisions, processes, and consequences (internal and external, positive or negative) of the business.

A corporation or company is a holon, an entity that lives by virtue of its constituent members, which are also holons. A company that seeks to maximize its quarterly financial picture at the expense of the physical, mental, emotional, or spiritual health and well-being of its customers—consciously or not—is not acting responsibly.

Because television is a service that has profound individual and social consequences, it's first responsibility is to viewers. Whatever the packaging, media messages are *experiences*, not products. They are memes, units of culture that convey meaning, express values, and contribute to the construction of our personal and social realities. Television is *formative*. What it *reflects* is not an objective reality, but an interpreted construct based upon social norms, agreements that are profoundly influenced by financial interests. Ratings in particular. Because television's messages and experiences can enflame terrorism on the one hand or activate altruism on the other, those who produce and distribute programming have a moral obligation to consider more than the financial ramifications of their offerings.

When profit is defined solely in monetary terms, a business can do anything it wants within the bounds of legality. But when the concept of profit is expanded to include the health and well-being of *all* stakeholders (viewers, employees, suppliers, administrators, owners, shareholders), the business positions itself for success across the board, not just in the board room.

Benefits this shift would bring—

- Increased stakeholder incentive to participate in the company's health and well-being
- Increased interest in the company undertaking a Governing Values Assessment (identity, purpose, mission) and operating with integrity to it
- Increased organizational vitality as a result of being part of a community that's moving in a beneficial direction, accomplishing common goals, and building for a sustainable future
- An increased sense of ownership by employees. This would result in greater creativity and productivity
- Increased sense of responsibility for the consequences of the company's offerings
- Increased productivity and quality because of the intrinsic (as well as extrinsic) benefits. Employees want their efforts to make a positive difference in their community or the broader world

PURPOSE

What are we here for? Why do we exist? What is our reason for being?

From: *Our purpose is to entertain and inform.*
To: *Our purpose is to help viewers realize their potentials and respond to change appropriately; healthy and vital individuals make a healthy and vital society.*

While entertainment is a value in itself, in the context of a mass medium it comes with a moral responsibility to do no harm. Entertainment can and sometimes does harm people and society. For example, "trash talk," glamorizing bad behaviors, sensationalizing gossip, depicting sex as love and ignorance as "cool," are not only offenses against human dignity and respect, they can be toxic for children and adolescents who are especially impressionable.

Stimulation and novelty have the higher purpose of helping individuals and communities adjust to change in ways that are appropriate to their health, well-being, and development. By holding the development, empowerment, and facilitation of human potential as a higher purpose, television can become a meaningful, socially responsible, and empowering resource.

Benefits this shift would bring—

- Viewers would consider television a *necessity* rather than a luxury, a resource well beyond but including the values of distraction, amusement, and window-on-the-world.
- Viewers would appreciate programs that are more responsive to their *authentic* and *higher* needs, wants, interests, and aspirations. Teachers, presenters, and performers in the areas of personal growth and social development would become celebrities.
- Television enterprises would become adept at identifying, monitoring, understanding, contextualizing, and reporting on the full spectrum of change. All kinds. All levels.
- Local television stations would want to become more involved in the lives of their viewers and local organizations. Understanding the true and higher needs, wants, and interests of viewers would improve the bottom line.
- As a result of providing more relevant, useful, and engaging programs and services, television stations would attract more segments of the non-viewing public and thereby increase profitability.

- By getting into the business of developing and producing programs that uplift, educate, inspire, engage, or empower, television channels and stations would particularize their brand image and attract aligned advertisers.

MISSION

What do we want to accomplish? What real value do we contribute?

From: *It's not our place to get involved in the lives of our viewers.*
To: *In large part we're here to contribute to the health and well-being of our viewers.*

The function of a socially responsible television enterprise is to participate collaboratively with its viewers in support of the optimization of their health, well-being, growth, and adjustment to change—and in the process create wealth.

A television network, channel, or station can do this by continuously informing its constituents about changes relevant to their lives and the larger whole systems in which they participate. This can be accomplished by informing, entertaining, and empowering viewers in ways that enrich and uplift as well as amuse, by identifying options and resources for constructive change, by facilitating discussions, dialogues, and events that encourage positive change, by initiating projects and events where meaningful interaction and positive outcomes can occur, and by empowering viewers to do more, be more, get more, have more, participate more and make more constructive changes in their lives, communities, and environments.

Benefits this shift would bring—

- By shifting the mission from self to other, community leaders and citizens would want to play an active role in shaping the content of programming and other television services. They could participate as volunteers, interns, consultants, advisors, or co-producers.
- Employees would appreciate the learning and creative opportunities that come from an expanded spectrum of communication services. They would also find increased satisfaction in work that's more meaningful, constructive, and useful—especially when they see positive results in the community.
- Stations would enjoy increased profitability from overall higher ratings, which come as a result of having an exceptional, specific, clear, and positive brand identity.

- Stations would enjoy increased profitability because sponsors would be eager to place their ads in real-value programming and services.
- Stations would enjoy increased profits from the packaging and syndication of low cost, original and thematic programming.
- Public service departments in stations would be substantially invigorated. They could develop additional revenue streams by providing content related publications, videos, workshops, social media assets, and promotional items.

BUSINESS STRATEGY

How do we accomplish our mission? What is the nature of our challenge?

From: *The challenge is to maximize they size of the audience for advertisers.*
To: *The challenge is to maximize substantive information and experiences for our viewers. This will deliver more desirable and better targeted viewers to even more advertisers.*

The strategy of delivering *real value* to customers is the key to increased profitability and long-term sustainability. MTV's business strategy has been to build *relationships* with their viewers and *engage* them in a *community of interest*. Their marketing people go to great lengths to understand their constituents so the company can respond to their authentic needs, wants, interests, and aspirations. They identify the trend-setters to determine what's likely to become "cool"—lingo, fashion, music, food and entertainment preferences. Rather than going for a sale, MTV's strategy is to create an ongoing transactional relationship with their highly targeted viewers. By doing so, their comparatively tiny market has delivered annual profits that exceed all the broadcast networks combined.

Viewers don't want to be sold a product or service. They want to come to it by choice and by participation in a cultural milieu, through memes. What has worked for the culture of rock music, can work for any other culture: dance, photography, fly-fishing, astronomy, football, quilting...

Benefits this shift would bring—

- By providing real-value, non-viewers would return to the screen and that would result in substantially increased market share.
- The television or cable enterprise would become a useful resources as well as a source of amusement.
- There would be increased consumer interest, attention, and participation.

- Viewers would be more inclined to join public conversations and participate in civic affairs.
- Sales would increase as a result of audience interest, diversity, and association with positive values. Advertisers would be eager to associate their brands and corporate images with content that's intelligent, constructive, inspirational, and empowering.
- As a brand, substantive programming would contribute to the revitalization of genres such as documentaries, historical dramas, self-help programs, meaningful talk, and event coverage.

SYMBIOSIS

How do we define success?

From: *We win by beating the competition.*
To: *We win by insuring that all our stakeholders win.*

In any given market, the quest to beat the competition by going head-to-head on conventional programming, particularly news, limits the branding and revenue potential for all its providers.

When the differentiating factor between local television stations is mainly the personality and appearance of anchorpersons, their packaging and promotion becomes the focus. The choice for viewers is similar to the choice between light red or dark red apples. Which set of personalities is more appealing and less annoying? By relying heavily on news doctors to advise them, news directors across the board have inadvertently homogenized and sanitized their offerings.

For instance, news consultants found that viewers pay more attention to stories that appear to be live rather than prerecorded and edited. As a result, every news operation in the nation began putting the word "live" on the screen as often as possible. For the same reason, lead stories are tagged, "exclusive" or "breaking," labels that in practice have little or nothing to do with the viewer's channel selection.

Far more likely to influence viewing choices would be to bookend the commercials before and after the newscast with only a brief interruption in the middle to separate news and weather from sports. Even better would be to alter the hiring criteria for anchors and reporters so that, beyond appearance and being able to read and write, journalists would be well connected in the community, have the ability to consistently make ethical decisions regarding story priorities, be able to articulate intelligent and insightful interpretations of the news, contextualize stories to help viewers *understand* their relevance and connection to their lives, and help them *appreciate* and not just be subjected to the news.

Ratings are a narrow, inaccurate, and self-serving means of evaluating a station's offerings. Even if the terms "live" and "breaking" were proven conclusively to attract viewers, is that *how* television stations want to attract their audiences? Is a news story any better, more relevant or significant in the lives of viewers by virtue of it happening now or being delivered first? At times, but rarely. Rather than being first to know what happened, wouldn't audiences prefer to have more details, greater accuracy, and expanded perceptions, even if it came a little later than other stations? Certainly, we want to know what happened as soon as possible. But to make *speed* the basis for promoting a newscast puts the proverbial cart before the horse.

In a media landscape populated with potentially hundreds of thousands of channels, viewers will be doing much less surfing and much more purposeful selection. In that environment, particularly if and when the economy tightens, people will increasingly be looking for substantive information and news they can use, along with television experiences that have a payoff beyond but including entertainment. Certainly we will continue to choose fluff. Mindless fare has its place, particularly in relieving stress and distracting us from everyday routines and challenges. But as life speeds up and becomes more complex, more people will be looking for more opportunities to learn, grow, and construct their best lives.

Benefits this shift would bring—

- By intention and design, everyone involved in and touched by mindful, meaningful, constructive, and empowering television content would win.
- Development, production, and distribution of substantive programming would provide real value to viewers. Substantive information is syntropic. Like land, it's a real "good." The fact that it's desirable, necessary, and scarce (rare on television), makes it intrinsically profitable.
- Viewer confidence would increase as a result of seeing that a network, station, channel, or web site is more interested in providing substance—programming that helps them live happier, healthier, more productive and fulfilling lives—than in besting the competition. This is essential for the health of the nation because, at base, money is a symbol of public

confidence. The greater the confidence in our institutions and corporations, the more secure the economy. (Television has yet to appreciate the extent to which it can and does influence the economy in this way).

- Competitors would increasingly become partners, collaborators in maximizing individual and social good. Instead of competing for dollars, they would compete for *opportunities* to become *distinctive* and thereby generate even more real value.
- Increasingly television writers, presenters, program developers, and journalists would be attracted to the company; the best people in the business want to be on the winning team, the cutting edge of innovation.
- Presenters who are intelligent and capable of articulating deeper and practical wisdom would become role models for our children.
- As a result of needing to understand the needs, wants, and circumstances of constituents, television providers would become more focused and involved in their communities. They would have increased incentive to discover what works in programming in response to continuously monitored and more accurately determined public demand, measured not only by the programs that are turned on, but by what turns people on and what they would *prefer* to watch.

CONSEQUENCES

What effect do we want to have on our customers?

From: *The road to market share and profits is to maximize affective stimulation.*
To: *The road to profitability and sustainability for all stakeholders is to provide real value, content that's meaningful, useful, inspirational, and empowering.*

This shift in thinking recognizes that television has major implications for society. Television impacts consciousness up and down the scale of holons: individuals, families, communities, societies, cultures, nations, the planet and species (Barker, 1989). In a capitalist society, television generates and stimulates wide-scale economic growth through competition. But when competition itself, rather than the exchange of real value becomes the driving force of a communications enterprise, public health and well-being can quickly become compromised. Rather than uplifting, inspiring and empowering viewers—and by extension contributing to a healthy and vital society—the battle over market-share drains them and depresses the spirit. Overexposure to breakdowns and people behaving badly saps both hope and growth. We turn inside and put up barriers to personal interaction, preferring to relate through electronic devices rather than face-to-face—the phenomenon social scientists refer to as "cocooning."

This is important in part, because our perceptions of each other, of life and its myriad realities are directly and profoundly influenced by self-fulfilling prophecy. Seeing contributes to believing. If we believe we are helpless, we act helpless. If we believe people are basically selfish, that's what we'll see and likely adopt. If we keep producing images of armageddon and telling stories of tragedy and abuse, they become normalized in our thinking and we come to expect, even worse accept them as they way things are. As we see, so we tend to create. What happens when the best in us is consistently overshadowed by the worst in us?

Benefits this shift would bring—

- Consideration of television's *consequences* from program design to delivery would empower professionals at all levels of the industry to identify and realize the medium's higher potentials.
- Increased public confidence in the future (which in many ways benefits the economy).
- A demand for more intelligent, self and socially-reflective programming.
- Television providers would be seen a valuable players in mental health, education, and social development.
- It would encourage the development, production, and distribution of programming that results in more positive and desirable viewer consequences.
- Self-fulfilling prophecy would shift from negative to balanced, perhaps even positive views of humanity and its future.

LEADERSHIP

As individuals and a company, how do we want to lead?

From: *Authoritative, top-down, command-and-control.*
To: *Collaboration and consensus. Leading by following the company's governing values.*

Genuine and inspiring leadership results in the empowerment of those being led. This kind of leadership requires caring, character, and consciousness as much as competence and daring, not only in business, but also in living. According to leadership theorist Warren Bennis, "Managers do things right; leaders do the right thing" (Bennis, 1989). Rather than imposing their will and ways, "servant" leaders attend to what's emerging (Greenleaf, 2002). They *care* about the total well-being of their constituents—all stakeholders.

Overriding personal gain and goals, autocratic leaders help the *team* get to where *it* wants to go. Sometimes just seeing team members thrive prompts the leader to act courageously on their behalf. An example is the CEO with a doctoral degree who proclaims and means: "If my washing the windows will move the company forward, that's what I want to do." It's the television general manager who says, "If constructive and meaningful programming is going to uplift the community and our staff, then that's the direction of our investment, and we'll find ways to do it so everyone benefits."

Benefits this shift would bring—

- A "leaderful" organization increases employee respect, confidence, and trust.
- There would be increased employee participation in and commitment to the company's governing values.
- Increased corporate flexibility would result from increased diversity and participation, making positive transformation relatively easy and quick.
- Company spirit and employee morale would soar due to increased ownership of the mission.
- The company would be invigorated with a sense of pride, both in the process and its targeted outcomes.

PROGRAM QUALITY AND VALUE

(From a producer's point-of-view) What do we hope for this project?

From: *I want this program to reach the largest audience possible.*
To: *I want this program to deliver real value to all who see it.*

A high quality, substantive television experience includes but transcends its methods of production, presentation, and presenters. Substance lies in the program's content, including its context and sub-text, and its implied but more often hidden agendas, intentions, and meanings.

Production formats, entertainment values, techniques, personalities, and presentation elements are all vital components, but they stand as *frame* in relation to the message—*what* is being communicated. A novel is not about the cover or the jacket blurb, the type style, or story structure. It's about the story itself, how it unfolds and what it conveys.

Substance on television makes the viewer want to call other people into the room to watch or phone a friend so they can watch. It compels us to take notes, record the program or afterward tell people about what we saw and discuss, not the editing, action, or the presenter and what she wore, but the message or experience that made an impact.

Anthropologist Gregory Bateson said about information that it "consists of differences that make a difference" (Bateson, 1988). *Data*, for instance the characters and words on this page, is inert and useless. But when organized in a certain way, data generates *information*, a mental construct or perception that makes a difference. Information becomes s*ubstantive,* of real value, when it can be used. To the extent that substantive information adds *value*, it increases in quality. "Cars were broken into last night." That's information. "Thieves are breaking into cars to steal CD players and GPS systems." That's substantive information. "Thieves have been targeting cars in the Pleasant Ridge area to get CD players and GPS systems. To prevent this from happening to you..." That's high quality, real value information. In this example the information helps viewers *avoid* a negative experience. Positive, substantive, and high quality information can also encourage, inspire, or empower positive responses.

Benefits this shift would bring—

- An emphasis on quality and value would be a *welcome* opportunity and creative challenge for television writers and producers.
- It would encourage the development, production, and distribution of programming that's both entertaining and substantial.
- It would raise the bar and contribute to the redefinition of "quality programming." The thinking would move from, "*Good programs are those people want to watch*," to "*Good programs are those people can't miss because they contain content that's important, useful, inspirational, or empowering*."
- The viewer's experience and conversations would be enriched and their perceptions expanded.

- Real-value programming would make self-fulfilling prophecy work *for* us rather than *against* us.
- Real-value programming would create productive partnerships between program developers and the intelligence community—scholars, scientists, researchers, teachers, and innovators in all fields.

DIFFERENTIATION

How are we distinctive? How do we differ from the competition?

From: *We produce and distribute programs that viewers want to see.*
To: *We are a source for knowledge, awareness, inspiration, and empowerment.*

Since the human capacity to create knowledge is infinite, and since knowledge grows when it's shared, the "knowledge-based organization" is better positioned for long-term survival and growth. What's more, it has increased capacity for both diversification and adaptation in a changing marketplace (Hock, 1999).

Benefits this shift would bring—

- The company would add *knowledge of* and *expertise in* particular subject areas to job descriptions relating to writing and program development.
- The company would fill positions with individuals who possess more knowledge and experience. An upgrade in the quality of human capital not only raises the quality of individual contributions, it improves the quality of every undertaking and vitalizes the corporate culture.
- Working partnerships would develop between program developers, producers and the intelligence community—scholars, scientists, researchers, teachers, and innovators.
- It would position the organization for long term growth and development.
- A broader definition of the information product—programming—would result in increased potentials for diversification, differentiation, branding, and marketing.
- Differentiation would position the company for long-term survival and growth. In lean times or when there's a threat to economic survival, a learning or knowledge oriented company is resilient, able to transform its structure and routines rather quickly.

Part IV

The Electronic Nervous System

5

Television As Nervous System

Many are realizing that the media are the nervous system of an evolving global consciousness. But to make that a wise global consciousness, the individuals who work in the media are going to have to find the core of their own personal integrity, and fend off the forces of survival and fear as motivating factors.

Peter Tjeerdsma

200,000 YEARS OF BIOLOGICAL EVOLUTION MAKES THE HUMAN nervous system an ideal model for the television industry because it constitutes the global body's primary communications network, conveying information throughout the system and activating appropriate responses to change at local, national, and global scales. This is why for many years social scientists, scholars, and authors in a variety of fields have and continue to use the analogy of the human nervous system to understand the role of the electronic media in society. Not surprisingly, as knowledge of the human nervous system grows, so do the parallels between it and the electronic media.

Economist Hazel Henderson observed that, "The sum of all channels of communication in a society makes up its vital nervous system" (Henderson, 1996). She views television networks, channels, and stations as the society's "primary integrative force," essential for turning the fragmented body politic into a healthy functioning whole. That being the case, she says the challenge of the media is "to ensure that all the components of this nervous system are free and open conduits for the maximum possible interchange of information between the maximum number of citizens." The internet has already accomplished this, and television is inexorably being drawn into it.

Social visionary Duane Elgin observed that, "Television, satellites, and computers are merging into an integrated, multimedia system and creating a central nervous system for the planet that is transforming every aspect of life" (Elgin, 1993). Richard P. Adler cites communication technologies and the media in particular as "psychomotor irritants, driving us, enticing us, to grow as a species. Television," he said, "is no less than our central nervous system" (Adler, 1981).

One of the main reasons for adopting the nervous system as a model for television's role in society, particularly considering its higher potentials in programming, is that television and the nervous system are holons, constituted of and composing higher-order living systems. In *Living Systems*, Dr. James Miller observed, "Composite entities made up of smaller living entities are also alive" (Miller, 1978). He demonstrated that cells, organs, organisms, groups, organizations, businesses, and societies are rightly classified as *living* systems because they are composed of living beings. However, because social systems such as universities, churches, corporations, and governments lack physical boundaries or membranes, they cannot be considered "organisms." Rather they are "ecosystems," collective life forms, living *environments* made up of communities of other, self-making, self-regulating, and interacting living beings.

Before moving on it's important to remember the distinction made earlier, that whereas mechanical systems have *parts*, living systems have *members*. Parts involve elements that are fixed and ordered, whereas members involve thinking entities who make choices. The cells that constitute biological bodies continuously make their own, individual choices. By exchanging energy and information, they change each other and their environments. It's these choice-making and information sharing characteristics that makes living beings and their collectives highly variable and chaotic in their behavior. This is keenly understood by anyone who has tried to influence or cohere a group of people.

So the television industry as a whole and each of its constituted networks, channels, and affiliated stations share a functional identity with the human nervous system. Each is a living ecosystem, an intercommunicating holon constituted of decision-making members who work together to provide their respective bodies with the information they need to maintain health, grow, and adjust to change.

THE FUNCTION OF A NERVOUS SYSTEM

Anthropologist Ashley Montagu observed, "The nervous system is functionally the stimulus-responding system of the organism" (Montagu, 1955). When the senses receive stimulation or impulses from the outside world, be they pleasurable, neutral, or painful, the nervous system *receives* the information, *interprets* the significance it might hold for the body and its members (by referencing memory), *processes* the nature, location, and magnitude of the stimulation, *compares* it against existing information, and *activates* a response. Nervous systems then, have evolved to sense, interpret, and activate so the organism can adjust to change appropriately. That's their purpose. Their function is to gather data, process it into information (differences that make a difference), and facilitate appropriate, life-sustaining and life-enhancing responses.

Any producer of electronic media reading Dr. Montagu's description of the nervous system's role in the physical body, could not help but see the many and direct correspondences to the television industry. For instance when he says that, "Cells and nerve fibers which comprise the human nervous system form an interconnecting network which links every part of the organism together," it evokes the image of television professionals and their related organizations forming a web of communication networks that link both professionals and viewers to their communities, nations, regions and world—and all of these to each other—within the context of a grand intercommunicating web.

Dr. Montagu is not alone in this assessment. Observe how the following statements made by a variety of neuroscientists (Partridge, 2003) apply to television functioning.

> "The most basic of nervous system characteristics, is excitability. All the other actions of the nervous system are dependent upon the results of excitation." (Stimulation)

> "Receptors, which are the input elements of the nervous system, change information into nerve signals. Effectors, the output elements of the nervous system, change these nerve signals into mechanical or chemical responses." (Journalist functions)

> "The nervous system controls processes that adjust both the internal operations of the individual, and relations between the individual and the external environment." (Newsrooms)

> "Normal neural functioning requires the combination of information entering over a period of time, and by way of multiple pathways." (Redundancy within and across channels)
>
> "A single nerve impulse on a single nerve fiber has little significance in neural functioning. Information must exist in combinations of impulses, and the nervous system must deal with these combinations." (Multiple sources of news and information)
>
> "We perceive a world whose dimensions are largely determined by the modalities of the specific sensory transducers that we possess." (Consciousness of television professionals)

Indeed, we perceive a world whose dimensions are largely (albeit not solely) determined by the family context, education, experiences, and perceptions of television writers, journalists, producers, and other culture-creators—storytellers. Television professionals functioning as transducers (information processors), transform data and perceptions into information, experiences, and stories, which become part of the collective reality and the collective unconscious. We call it *culture*. What's important to remember is that all these perceptions are *constructions*, and they come to us *interpreted* through the lenses of personal histories, interests, philosophies, values, and experiences. It bears emphasis: exposure to any communications medium is exposure to the *consciousness* of its creator. For those who can see between the pixels, television mainly reveals the consciousness of its producers—their perceptions, values, preferences, and agendas.

So what does the nervous system model contribute to this quest to understand television's *higher* potentials? It suggests that the industry, together with all its sub-holons, has a fundamental purpose that has only in part been realized, and that with few exceptions, television has more and far greater capacities than convention has allowed.

Ashley Montagu (Anthropologist and humanist):

> "The purpose of a nervous system is to adjust the parts of the body to one another and to the body as a whole, so the organism can adjust to its environment appropriately."

APPLYING THE MODEL TO TELEVISION

Because the relationship between the human body and its nervous system closely parallels the relationship between the social body and the television industry, the nervous system model provides insight into television's more organic and responsible functioning. It's especially appropriate considering the industry derives its power in large part by appealing to the biological and emotional needs of its constituent viewers.

While further applications of the model will be discussed in the area of programming, some of the implications for television businesses are appropriate to specify here, particularly in light of the paradigm of interconnection. The nervous system model suggests that—

- One employee's function is not more important or better than any other. Every "cell," each individual, is important and needed.
- The strongest and most effective teams are those made up of *diverse* individuals having *complementary* skills so each member can contribute and uniquely create rather than duplicate. If all the members of a football team were skilled quarterbacks, they'd never win a game. A symphony requires many and diverse instruments, not all reeds or horns.
- Employees function best when their role matches their nature, their deepest understanding of themselves and their reason for being. A heart cell will never be content doing the work of a liver cell. Discontent is toxic.
- Departments and divisions are not discrete, separate entities. They are interconnected and interdependent components of a whole system. Their common function is to collaborate to produce systemic health and well-being at the higher level.
- Throughout the organization there needs to be frequent and effective communication. A body cannot function optimally when its constituent members are out of the loop. It leads to dysfunction and the energy expended is counterproductive.
- Member cells are both constituents and stakeholders. They are the "receptor cells" of the social body, and they are adjusting to change moment to moment. Their collective behavior ("demand" in business terms) directly and dramatically influences the state of the whole body. It's not just that viewers *can* affect change. They are the *agents* of change.

- Life itself has been characterized as change. Everything everywhere is constantly changing. And change precipitates responses. Adjustment. The proper and higher role of television is to help its constituents respond to change *appropriately*—in ways that safeguard and promote their health and well-being, growth and aspiration.
- In healthy living systems, individuals take responsibility for themselves *and* the higher-level holons within which they are members. Both. Together. Never one without the other. Health, defined as harmony or balance, requires cooperation. Not competition. Liver cells do not disadvantage kidney cells in order to survive. The eyes have no interest in becoming better at providing data to the brain than do the ears—unless one of these organs is impaired. A television station is not "better" or "worse" than any other. Each should provide programming and services unique to and building upon, their governing values.

BROADER IMPLICATIONS OF THE MODEL

In recent years, references to the electronic media as a nervous system have increased substantially. In addition to making this connection, contemporary thinkers in a variety of fields are pointing to its implications.

Television Shapes Reality and Culture

In *Corporate DNA: Learning from life*, Ken Baskin draws many and substantial parallels between the human nervous system and corporations (Baskin, 1998).

Ken Baskin (Business consultant):

> "(Nervous systems) *integrate* a picture of our world for us, tell us which pieces of information we should pay attention to, helps us *interpret* that information, *monitors* our health and internal systems, *coordinates* body-wide activity, and *makes decisions* for the whole." (Italics mine).

Some might question the last part of this statement—whether a television enterprise should make decisions for the social body, but in practice that's what television writers and producers do. By selecting, prioritizing, interpreting, and packaging information and experiences, they are make *assumptions about* and *decisions for* their viewers. Television journalists and meteorologists decide when to release important, potentially life-saving information. Talk show hosts and their producers decide which topics are important and how they will be presented. Interviewers manipulate their conversations so interviewees give them the response, or the kind of reaction they want. Referencing and interpreting research data, programmers ultimately make decisions based on what *they* think will attract and hold the target audience's attention. The same is true for writers and producers of documentaries, sit-coms, and hour-long dramas. Decisions are constantly being made on behalf of the public.

Like our personal realities, culture is not a legacy of the past. It's a moment-to-moment *construct*, which in today's media-saturated environment is largely shaped by those who attract and hold our attention. Eminent professor of media communication, Dr. George Gerbner, observed that, "Whoever tells most of the stories to most of the people most of the time has effectively assumed the cultural roles of parent and school" (Gerbner, 1981). Television has and still holds the title in this regard. Add to this the fact that, "More Americans get their news from television than from any other source." The implication: Whether we are aware of it or not, whether we watch a lot of television or none at all, individually and collectively, by performing the functions of a nervous system, television is one of the most powerful forces in constructing both our personal and social realities.

With Great Power Comes Great Responsibility

As a complex of nested nervous systems—internet, radio, television networks, channels, and stations and their program providers—the electronic media play a unique role in the life of humans and the planet. They stand in the middle as informers, storytellers, interpreters, and motivators. The public's implied contract with the media is that, in exchange for attention, the industry will deliver a modicum of truth, accuracy, intelligence, ethical behavior, and entertainment experiences. In short, we expect them to act responsibly, in our best interest.

To accomplish their mission, the mass media are accorded privileged access to information and resources across all levels and departments of society. Doors that are closed to the public are open to them. But with this privilege comes at least two specific responsibilities associated with nervous system functioning. The first is to operate in ways that continuously and vigorously safeguard the health and well-being of its member cells. The second is to continuously and rigorously earn our trust. If a media corporation or company is to operate responsibly, with integrity to its constituency and in keeping with its governing values, it must attend to its own health, well-being, and appropriate adjustment.

As the number of thinking cells on the planet increase, and the web of their interrelations expands and becomes more complex and interconnected, the whole of humanity is becoming more intelligent, interdependent, and self-reflective.

Duane Elgin:

> "The ability to witness our own knowing represents a powerful evolutionary advance because it enables us to take charge of our social development with a new level of clarity and intentionality" (Elgin, 1993).

On occasion, television provides glimpses of enormous crowds, people in numbers so great that, in those moments, we get a taste of the immensity of the human family. Rarely however, do we get to experience the depth and grandeur of what's inside the human mind, heart, and spirit. Who for instance, and where are the contemporary equivalents of St. Francis, Leonardo de Vince, Madam Curie, Michelangelo, Pocahontas, Galileo, Gandhi, Einstein, Henry Ford, Rosa Parks? Who and where are today's saints, seers, and innovators? Where do we see people realizing their fuller potentials? Where are the models of cooperation, compassion, and true love?

In the interest of maximizing its audience, conventional television tends to be *reactive* with a propensity toward the *sensational*. Events such as hurricane Katrina, the Haiti catastrophe and Japan's tsunami seem to indicate that it takes a major disaster for people to wake up, to join together in common purpose and transcend the limitations of the physical. Sometimes it takes a disaster. But in addition to having nervous systems that help us respond to change personally, human beings are also endowed with reflection and foresight. Whatever the cause, we can learn from tragedy and breakdown, even take preventative and preparatory measures to reduce, at least to some extent, the frequency and severity of violent change.

News programs show us what happened and dramatic productions show us the dangers of what could happen, but there's also an opportunity for television to be proactive. *Extreme Makeover: Home Edition* is an excellent example of this, responding positively to negative circumstances. By putting out calls for assistance and facilitating the construction of homes, people's lives and whole communities are renewed and invigorated. In the process viewers are uplifted and inspired by these demonstrations of caring, altruism, and cooperation

(Endemol USA, 2006). Each episode creates a win for everyone at all levels. It shows what can be done when media professionals take an active role as facilitators of positive change.

It also shows that the industry is already populated with thinking and caring individuals, providing for the possibility that more of television could be *proactive* with propensities toward *intelligence, wisdom*, and *caring*—so viewers can see and know that breakdowns and tragedies can be effectively prevented or managed.

Truth

Biological nervous systems present the truth of a situation to the whole body and to the fullest extent possible. True and accurate information is essential for maintaining the health and well-being their host bodies. This also applies to electronic nervous systems. Television has a responsibility to provide accurate, true, and complete pictures of what's happening that is or may be important to its host body. Viewers.

What information and which experiences are important to communicate? Anything and everything that can or could potentially affect, positively or negatively, the health and well-being of individual cells, their communities, or their higher level holons. It's a challenging responsibility. But there's no getting around it: health, harmony, and balance require information that's as true and complete as possible. And because living systems are interconnected and interdependent, responsibility applies to the levels above and below. Considered from the top down, a healthy planet requires healthy nations, corporations, communities, families, and individuals.

Bias

Nervous systems are necessarily biased. They advocate and seek the health and well-being of their host bodies and their constituent cells. They warn of breakdowns, send signals to the brain to stop dysfunctional behaviors, and they send preventative and healing emissaries—immune cells—to locations where there are potential or real threats, traumas, or injuries.

Understandably, to avoid lawsuits, television executives have learned to be extremely cautious. They choose not to openly display a bias, even for positive values, for fear of ruffling someone's feathers. But nervous systems are courageous. They stand up and take a position unapologetically. They activate positive responses. And they do no harm. For nervous systems, facilitating appropriate adjustments to change is "job one."

This is not to advise recklessness. The nervous system model suggests that the standards against which programming and content are measured should include consideration of the *consequences* for viewers, including the holons above and below them.

CONCLUSION

A nervous system keeps its member cells informed about changes within and beyond the host body so they can respond in ways that maintain and ideally promote its health and well-being. Unless the change presents a real threat to the system, a responsible nervous system does not shock the cells in order to get their attention. Neither does it distract them from what they need to know or do, no matter how difficult or challenging the message. It communicates as much of the truth as it can grasp, maintaining moment-to-moment focus on the message itself rather than the messenger or delivery mechanism.

A nervous system is neither neutral nor passive. It is positive and proactive. It has a vested interest in maintaining the health and well-being of each and every cell because their condition determines the condition of the whole body—including the members of the nervous system.

6

Governing Values Assessment

The soul of an enterprise bonds it together as one force giving it identity, purpose, direction and a reason for being... Many pooh-pooh the reality and value of soul in the corporate world but it is truly amazing how, given the same business circumstances, some companies do so much better than others. It is not soul that assures success, but it is the presence of soul that unifies the mission to achieve success... Companies with soul never lose sight of one thought – If you are not making history, you are history!

Bob MacDonald

GOVERNING VALUES ARE THE CORE IDEAS ABOUT AN ENTITY that keep it on track and steer it toward a specified destination. The reason for specifying these values in a series of statements is to have in writing a definition of the company that makes its self-regulation function meaningful and effective. Once completed, the document becomes the internal governor that recommends policies and behaviors which are focused and consistent at the level of the individual parts so the whole has the best chance of arriving at the intended, rather than a random or undesirable, destination. Like the American constitution, a statement of governing values provides an ongoing and tangible reference to an entity's clearest definition of itself, its ideals, functions and aspirations.

A Governing Values Assessment "package" constitutes a company's DNA, the essential and unique codes that make it what it is. If revenue is the engine that powers a business, the governing values are its blueprints, engineering design, and rudder all rolled into one document.

GOVERNING VALUES ASSESSMENT PACKAGE

Identity
Defines the entity as a unique being

Purpose
Specifies the entity's reason for being

Mission
Specifies the activity that will fulfill the entity's purpose

Strategy
Specifies how the entity will carry out its mission

Vision
Specifies the destination and milestones

Values
Specifies the values that will guide all of the above

The practice of creating and periodically assessing governing values is as important for individuals as it is for start-up companies and well established organizations or corporations. In the interest of focus, the identity, purpose, and mission statements should be limited to one sentence. If a word isn't necessary, eliminate it. If a word doesn't feel quite right, find a better one. Accuracy and truth. No fluff, explanations, or embellishment. In all the statements, consider the verbs most carefully. Nuances make a huge difference when it comes to describing action. For instance, the difference between "instruct," which relates to teaching someone *skills*, and "educate," which relates to conveying *knowledge*. They're not the same thing.

In the Mission Statement, realize that although there may be several activities that will fulfill the purpose, each added activity tends to diminish the effectiveness of the others. As inclined as we are to multitasking, human beings and their collectives can accomplish one thing *extremely* well together. They can accomplish two things *quite* well—three things *adequately*, four things *poorly*, five things *badly*. The key is to limit and prioritize! Focus and distinction increase as mission-related activities are minimized. When the process is complete a document is produced, shared widely, and used as guidelines for making and implementing decisions at every level.

Part V

Television's Higher Potentials

7

Enriching And Expanding Television's Capacities

Our mass media are only a poor shadow of what they could be—not for lack of technology, but because of our imperfect understanding of their potential power.

Hazel Henderson

CURRENTLY, PROGRAMMING CAPACITIES IN THE BROADCAST sphere focus on news, information, and entertainment. When cable systems came along the definition of these categories expanded somewhat, particularly in the news and information arenas which saw the development of 24-hour news channels and special interest channels, largely running in parallel with specialized newsstand magazines. These were mostly *developmental* rather than *evolutionary* advances. More of the same. There's still plenty of room for innovation within these categories, but there are entire categories and capacities yet to be explored. Before we consider these additional capacities and provide examples, consider how even the conventional offerings have room to grow.

REPORTING

Apart from political content, conventional news operations focus on what's going wrong in the world and in people's lives: stories of personal tragedy, social breakdown, and global disaster. The expanded definition of what's worthy to report now includes, "How to" tips regarding appearance, food and diet, exercise and beauty, time and stress management. Celebrity news and gossip has expanded to whole channels. And consumer news is a common feature. Predictably, "hard news" (news that's hard to hear) presentations conclude with a human interest story that allows for some pleasant or comedic banter to end the program on a lighter note.

Well and good. But there's much to report that rarely, if ever, gets into the mainstream pipelines. First and foremost among these is positive content to balance the negative. The result of a nervous system that continuously and exclusively reports on breakdowns and threats, is a body-mind system that, because it lives in fear, holds a negative view of life and is mostly in a reactive and regressive mode. What's needed are stories of personal and social triumph, stories of accomplishment, success, breakthrough, transformation, discovery, celebration, and knowledge gained. Especially, we need stories that present positive *models* of health and healthy relationships, integrity, wisdom, effective collaboration, caring, nurturing, and altruism. Other possibilities include—

- What's working in education, technology, business, the nonprofit as well as private sectors
- Profiles of emergents (identified earlier), social innovators whose thought and action is enriching, productive, and fulfilling for themselves and others
- Entrepreneur profiles: their projects, visions, progress, and needs
- Eco-newscasts: Who's doing what locally to raise awareness and improve the environment?
- Community improvement initiatives that match needs and resources
- Good works needing funding or sponsorship; grant writing; volunteerism; collaborations
- Community histories with profiles of the people who made it
- Coverage of local conferences, workshops, and symposia that focus on content rather than presenters or performers
- International perspectives: What other cultures are getting it right and contributing to the world
- Single-story newscast: In context and in-depth stories that are relevant to the community

INFORMING

Whereas conventional television tends to focus on new information and present it in capsule forms such as tips and trivial, all-too-brief segments on morning talk shows, the field is wide open to provide substantive content and in ways that do justice to the topic. Gregory Bateson's definition of information as a difference that makes a difference provides a useful guide to developing content that truly informs. Any information, be it old or new, as long as it contributes to health, well-being, efficiency, effectiveness, creativity, understanding, aspiration, imagination, or meaning holds potential for creating programming that matters.

It's easy to assume that viewers know what we, as producers, know. Or that they don't need or want to know what we know. Not so. Producers eager for a creative challenge and an opportunity to make a difference need only ask: What information would make the lives of our audience easier, better, more creative, productive, prosperous, comfortable, satisfying, or fulfilling? (The list goes on.)

ENTERTAINING

We are entertained by activities or performances that amuse, hold or divert our attention, give pleasure, or provide relaxation. The television and cable industries have become so successful at entertaining that they and the viewing public consider it to be television's primary function. It's why most people purchase a TV set. Although it can be difficult to see at times, the vast majority of programs, irrespective of content and format, attempt to entertain as they inform, promote and sell. Even the news.

And that's understandable, particularly when the industry "winners" are considered to be those who come out ahead in the ratings. The key to success in a *mass* medium is very straightforward: provide entertainment that appeals to the masses—easy to watch, sensational fare, controversy, violence and power struggles, sex and glamour, gossip, trash-talk, outrageous behavior, trivia, revved up give-aways, and "reality" competitions that bring out the worst in people. As noted, this too is understandable. In the deep past, being on the lookout for such things had survival value.

On the next turn of the spiral, there could well be a resurgence of, or innovations in some of the former popular genres including live comedy (*The Carol Burnett Show, The Steve Allen Show*), variety shows (*Ed Sullivan, Your*

Show of Shows, Sonny & Cher, Hee Haw), star performer series' (*I Love Lucy, Andy Griffith, The Honeymooners*), and situation comedies (*All In The Family, Mary Tyler Moore Show, Cheers, Friends*). As classics, they carry a message for aspiring and creative writers: Audiences are entertained, not by one-liners and posturing, but by unique and talented personalities, people who reflect or celebrate the human condition with all its ups and downs, flavors and textures, in the context of real life situations. And performers who make us laugh, feed our souls, or rock our world.

Innovation in these areas begin and end with people *being* funny. (*Everybody Loves Raymond, The Cosby Show, Mad About You, Frazier*). American audiences are consistently entertained by unique personalities, people who are fascinating to watch by virtue of their amusing behaviors and how they talk.

Beyond the prospect of revitalizing classic pathways to entertain, there are other capacities awaiting development suggested by the field of psychology. For instance, we love to watch lovers. Not just people *in* love with other people, but people *loving* what they do—or loving some aspect of their lives. People pursuing a passion are fascinating to watch because we want that experience for ourselves, and for a moment we can live their quest vicariously. Empathic love is both contagious and motivating.

Another capability indicated by psychology grows out of our desire for community. We long for connection, even if means fantasizing for an hour what it would be like to be part of a tight-knit group of people. *Friends, Seinfeld, and Cheers,* fed these desires in a comedic way. *Northern Exposure, Gilmore Girls, The West Wing, and The Good Wife* provided access to more serious but equally tight communities. The desire for connection that's both *intimate* and *enjoyable* is universal. Stories that invite us into those kinds of communities—whether five or fifty people—will never be out of fashion.

Writers and producers looking for programming concepts that feature entertainment will find them readily in two places: in psychology textbooks and in their own families. Pay particular attention to the family and spousal interactions you find annoying. Instead of participating in your role as father, mother, spouse, friend or other, assume the role of audience and consider the *universal* aspects of the situation. When writing, exemplify and exaggerate the situation, create unique personalities, a plausible context for their interaction, and have it all happen in a setting that's fascinating in itself.

ENGAGING

A significant function of a nervous system is *activation*. It doesn't just gather, interpret, and report. It facilitates cellular communication and interaction.

Lend A Hand

"TV Five anchors John Jones and Karen Gray will be picking up litter in the Pleasant Hill area. You're invited to join them (details provided). Those who participate will be given a complimentary pass to a Cincinnati Red's baseball game. John and Karen will be wearing baseball uniforms, so dress accordingly. (Such & Such restaurant) will provide hot dogs and beverages along the five-mile walk. All ages are welcome..."

Going Public

A team of journalists approach everyday people and ask what they'd like to see improved in their community or workplace. The producer invites them to make it happen. The producer and camera crew go with these citizens to an appropriate location to better understand the challenge and consider solutions. In some instances the collaboration will produce solutions. If not, viewers will understand the complexities and differing perspectives involved. For instance, a mother who wants better after school options for her children, prompts a team to identify a situation that works for them. If none are found, they approach community administrators and business managers to see if they could help create an option that works.

Project Profile

An experienced grant-writing expert profiles local projects and the people leading them. The program is live with on location, pre-produced packages that have the project director and other principals describe the project and provide background including their motivation, vision, design, challenges, successes, research, resources, current status, and needs. Viewers call in or text their comments, ideas and suggestions. The projects and proposals considered are those that will benefit individuals and the community: art and media, development initiatives, environmental solutions, neighborhood improvement, health, education, vocational training.

(Your City's Name): Making A Difference

After weeks of promotion, a diverse anchor team hosts a live, citywide celebration. In advance of the air date, the producers invite 100 citizens to come together to make a difference in the community. Five teams of twenty individuals are selected to represent the full diversity of the city. At the first meeting these people meet one another and the program hosts facilitate a process where each team selects a leader. The leaders then coordinate their teams, each receiving a monetary stipend from the station or a local business sponsor.

The team process begins with the first televised program, which is broadcast live with viewers contributing ideas and suggestions. Afterward, the teams design their projects based upon a provided list of community's priorities and viewer recommendations. Roles are assign. The Chamber of Commerce and other professional organizations enlist the support of the business community. Corporate sponsors provide food and resources: tools, materials, equipment. Smaller companies volunteer personnel. Viewers donate professional services and skills. Cameras follow the teams into the community to see how their plans are being implemented. This provides content for the next program. Enthusiasm builds due to the outpouring of support. The presence of cameras opens doors that otherwise would be closed. Throughout the project, team members are profiled on television in promos so viewers have a "cast of characters" to care about, root for and support.

Broadcast live with an audience, the final program is a celebration of team accomplishments: Team One conducted a series of highly targeted workshops in nutrition, conflict resolution, empowerment, and employment. In support of Team Two, a leading food chain donated three tractor-trailers filled with tons of groceries for the food bank; area restaurants kicked off the give-away with a feast served by police officers wearing jeans and black ties; professional baseball and basketball players demonstrate their skills and play hoops with attending kids. Team Three refurbished an elementary school building. Team Four demolished a building being used by drug dealers and replaced it with a well-lit green space and playground with a basketball court. Using a fleet of vehicles provided by area hospitals, Team Five provided health and counseling services in the inner city using volunteer medical professionals. The teams are acknowledged by the mayor and the sponsors. Corporate sponsors lavish the participants with gifts and opportunities. The project is so successful City Council decides to make it an annual summertime event.

ENRICHING

Television has made and continues to make our lives richer by providing access to the full spectrum of music and performing arts. PBS has been an exemplar in this area, but this remains an area rich with possibilities for innovation.

The Web Of Life

This highly visual TV magazine consists of departments hosted by science experts adept at communicating complex ideas simply. Animated graphics supplement on location and laboratory images. Departments include ecology, astronomy, biology, chemistry, and physics. The hosts are more than ringmasters. Their role is to integrate the topics across the sciences so viewers can see how everything is related and interconnected in the web of life.

The Grand Contributors

Highly respected "contributors" in a variety of fields present a talk on a topic of their choosing. An ideal time to air such a program would be around lunchtime on weekdays so working people could sit together, watch, and discuss the content. These oratories are pre-recorded so relevant B-roll images can be incorporated. As happened in ancient Greece, exposure to intelligence, vision, and wisdom would raise the level of public discourse and provide models for logic and reasoning.

Blue Sky Coffee Shop

This often humorous series features a group of people who are lovers of ideas. They come together weekly in a coffee shop to sit with the owner who has a passion for discussing ideas. We get to know these people very well. It's a community, but unlike *Friends*, these people are not actors. Other visitors (patrons) are invited to participate, so each week there are new people—writers, teachers, students, artists, visionaries, book and media people.

In this context we oversee partly prepared but mostly *spontaneous* and *spirited* discussions on a wide variety of topics, usually social and artistic issues and concerns beyond the realms of politics and popular culture (which are already out there.) The subject matter is announced and promoted in advance so the participants, some of whom will be celebrities, come to the coffee shop well prepared. Since viewers know the thematic content in advance, they can phone-in or email their contributions.

EDUCATING

Early forays into "educational television" failed because producers approached it like school—teachers imparting information by talking to the camera. *Educaré*, the Latin word for "raising up," means nurturing, filling up. And that requires much more than access to data or information. The higher purpose of education is the development of mental and moral *capacities*: articulation, making value judgments, discernment, critical thinking, ethics. As well as securing a job, education is about personal growth, enrichment, and preparation for responsible citizenship. It's about understanding the lessons of the past, right relationship, increasing awareness of self and the world. And creating meaning.

According to cosmologist Brian Swimme and ecologist Thomas Berry, "The primary purpose of education should be to enable individual humans to fulfill their proper role in the larger pattern of meaning—the universe story. We can understand our role in the Great Story only if we know the story in its full dimensions (Swimme, 1994)." Environmentalist Lester Brown spells it out for the media: "The communications industry is the only instrument that has the capacity to educate on a scale that is needed and in the time available."

What is needed—and quickly—are compelling and entertaining programs and segments, even one-minute spots that approach three particular aspects of education. First, correct and update the inaccurate information in every field that is being taught in schools at all levels. (Columbus was not the first to discover America. Genes are not fatal sentences to illness. "Survival of the fittest" applies only in certain situations. And the mind is a property of the whole body, not just the brain). Second, is the need for leading-edge knowledge across all disciplines to be disseminated to the wider public. Who's doing what, where, why, how, and what are they learning? Finally, the public needs access to models of learning and education that are working. How do we learn best? What are the best ways to develop awareness, critical thinking skills, and moral conviction? What can a parent do to recognize and help realize their child's potentials at various stages?

Beyond that, what can corporations do to educate their employees so they are more creative, responsible, engaged, and productive? Where are there opportunities in the community and beyond, for learning to be accelerated? What scholarships go begging every year—and why? What are the personal qualities that contribute to teaching excellence? What are the environmental factors that contribute to learning? What are the qualities of a good school administrator?

INSPIRING

As part of their activation function, electronic nervous systems have the capacity to inspire, to spark fresh ideas and stimulate the urge to create. There are instances where television is already doing this, but such programs are rare. What would it be like if writers and producers *began* with the intent to uplift, inspire, or empower their viewers?

Lovers

(As noted in the text) Rather than stories about people in love with each other, these love stories are about people who have a passion for something that enriches their lives. It could be an intellectual or creative pursuit, a type of work, lifestyle, role, or sport. Passionate people are not content to simply engage the subject of their attraction, they immerse themselves in the details. Classic cars, railroading, baking, embroidery, photography, gardening, painting, dancing, writing, music.

Living Green

Profiles of people who have found ways to live well and minimize their carbon footprint. These people may be living off the grid, doing organic gardening, buying less at the grocery store, building structures that minimize upkeep and energy or converting natural substances to fuel. Whether they have discovered one little innovation, such as building a better compost bin or a self-sufficient house, their enthusiasm inspires viewers to assess their own environmental circumstances to see what they can to live a more green lifestyle.

Eye On Nature

This program exposes viewers to exquisite nature images made by world-class photographers. The images would be shot in high-definition video. The audio would be all natural sounds—no music or narration. The beauty of the natural world, well composed and edited into thematic sequences would be inspiration enough. Many of the scenes would be aerial images, but there would also be a full range of tripod-setups, satellite images, and live-motion images taken through telescopes and microscopes.

EMPOWERING

Another aspect of television's activation function is the capacity to empower, to move viewers not only to identify their potentials, but to help realize them by gaining the skills and knowledge they need to overcome obstacles and develop self-confidence so they can live their best lives and contribute their unique gifts.

The Path

Charismatic experts in a variety of fields present their perspectives, tools, techniques, and models of success to empower viewers to identify their own potentials and put into practice the thinking and behaviors that have been shown to transform, increase performance, overcome limitations, and attain fulfillment. Although the experts may or may not subscribe to Buddhism, the program's segments derive from the Buddha's eightfold path: right view (perception), right intention, right speech, right action, right livelihood, right effort, right mindfulness, and right concentration.

Motherhood

It may seem that there are no perfect mothers, but there are many women who are raising happy and well-adjusted children. Each self-narrated program features one of these mothers, a woman who is considered by psychologists and parenting authors to be doing a good job with their children. The program provides models, information, and techniques on effective parenting, discussions on parent and child attitudes, behavior, crisis management, childhood development, illness, and temperament.

Corporate Heights

On location in the nation's top 100 corporations, viewers are introduced to an employee who participates in the application of a technique or process designed to maximize his or her effectiveness—individually and as a member of a team. The processes derive from those introduced by leading business gurus. For instance we follow employees through meetings and trainings such as: building synergy, rings of empowerment, resonating core dynamics, six-sigma, transactional analysis, brainstorming, envisioning, rotating leadership. The programs conclude with a follow-up segment to show and celebrate the benefits gained.

Emily Green

In this hour-long dramatic series, Emily is just out of college. Her major was Art History. She's a no nonsense rebel. Once she bites into a project, she never lets go. Unable to find work, circumstances land her in a dangerous inner-city neighborhood seeking shelter with homeless people. In each episode we watch her pull herself up by sheer grit. Standing her ethical ground, she transforms those around her by discovering their unique talents and empowering them by example. The drama consists of Emily continuously turning tragedy into triumph. It's the story of an ordinary young woman doing extraordinary things by being observant, compassionate, industrious, and determined. As the series progresses we see her neighbors and the neighborhood transforming.

FACILITATING

As we observed, nervous systems facilitate appropriate responses to change, particularly when the change presents a threat to the body's security or health. An important part of *appropriate* responding—maintaining or contributing to health and well-being—involves communicating potential or actual threats to the members of the body who would be or are impacted by the change, and then facilitating their interaction with the body's health regulating systems toward the adoption of responses that will restore balance and harmony.

Because it's role in the body is communication, the nervous system's activation function primarily involves *facilitation*. It does not initiate change. Neither does it force it. It presents the appropriate members of its host body with accurate and true information about what's happening and facilitates their interaction so the body as a whole can respond appropriately. The *activation* function of a nervous system is as critical to the health of the body as are the *sensing* and *interpreting* functions.

Local television newsrooms are already adept at gathering data and transforming it into information that's interpreted, edited, and reported to the social body. But for the flow of information and energy to end there would be like a nervous system informing its host that a finger is burning and then ignoring it, moving on to look for a threat that's more dramatic. While it's not appropriate for *newsrooms* to convene and facilitate interaction among community members to respond to threats, it is appropriate for the *company* to do so because it's one of the primary members of the body charged with the communication function. Because the television station has the means, expertise, and charter to inform the community, it also has the responsibility to convene as warranted, those affected by significant events and facilitate on and off-air conversations and dialogues to consider appropriate responses and make recommendations to those empowered to affect change.

Talk show hosts who perceive their job as primarily entertaining and getting high ratings are not the people to do this. It takes trained communication *specialists*, those qualified to facilitate formal dialogue that's respectful and productive, safeguarding the integrity of the relationships involved.

When the nightly news displays a *pattern* of breakdowns within the community such as an increase in drug crime, this "Special Communications Unit" would take it as a sign that the social body is in need of attention in this area, and do whatever it can to see that it gets that attention. For the Communications Unit this means researching, networking, coordinating, convening, and hosting.

Because part of the activation function is insuring that learning has occurred throughout the body, the outcomes of the facilitation process need to be communicated to the entire community—and not as a series of mere conversations. "Talking heads" are deadly on television. There are many creative options, one of which would be a well produced documentary featuring a highly respected member of the community as host. Ideally, this person would be part of or lead the Special Communications Unit. The documentary would need to be heavily promoted and include elements that would draw viewers to the screen.

Who pays for all this? The company. It's part of being a responsible member of the community. The payoffs? It fulfills public service licensing requirements. Also, a demonstration of social responsibility such as this, particularly if it becomes a pattern, is likely to return profits in terms of increased advertising, improved brand recognition, increased audience respect and loyalty, perhaps even national recognition by providing a model of how television can make a positive difference in the community. In addition to whatever successes might be achieved by the facilitation process itself, the payoff for the company would be the satisfaction that comes from serving its host body—the community—as a responsible nervous system.

Mining The Core

A producer with a passion for social harmony goes into the homes of everyday people to gather diverse, non-partisan, well thought-out perspectives on core values—consumerism, environment, big/small government, health care, drugs, mental health. The interviews are edited to include statistics, which are presented graphically, and perspectives from experts (other than politicians) experienced in the topic. The tacit goal of the program is to facilitate public conversation on core values as a way to understand the causes of valuing; to promote tolerance and respectful discourse.

Nexus

A weekly program which facilitates connection to —

Self: A segment that features self-help experts who facilitate personal growth through physical, mental, and spiritual exercises.

Interests: Profiles, call-in, text to connect viewers to other people, experts, and resources (databases, literature, gatherings, jobs, supplies) pertaining to a wide variety of fields and topics from hobbies to career tracks.

Events. A "Calendar of Events" segment relating to a wide variety of special interests.

Opportunities. An "Opportunities Hotline" where viewers learn about jobs or opportunities to volunteer their time, offer services, or work on projects in their area of interest.

Information: A segment on where to find information on the internet; telephone applications, databases, specialized libraries, corporate and government sources.

Solutions

Announcer voice-over news footage: "Three weeks ago we reported an alcohol-related incident that took the lives of two Central High School students. (Details). In an effort to prevent further violence in our schools, Channel Four is inviting you to participate in an open and facilitated, on-air dialogue. We want to hear your views on the underlying causes of violence in our schools, and to identify workable solutions. The governor, mayor, city officials, school board, and psychologists will be available for Q&A. Soon after the air date, a task force will be charged with implementing the solutions that have the best likelihood of success. XYZ Corporation will provide food and beverages for the dialogue. All participants will receive complimentary passes to (a concert, sporting event or other). (Details)

SHOWCASING

Like the human body, a social body that's routinely fed a diet of negative information can quickly become depressed and disempowered. With incomplete and a narrow perceptions of itself, it eventually succumbs to self-fulfilling prophecy and the problems intensify. Health requires a balanced view of self, one that says: "I may have problems, but I am good and strong enough to handle what comes along. I can adapt to this situation and do so gently, rather than traumatically."

In addition to pointing to weaknesses and breakdowns in the community that call for facilitation, an electronic nervous system can also inject the social body with a positive self-image to bolster confidence by showcasing strengths and what's going right.

Stories that evidence individual and collective strength can be found in virtuous behavior, technological advancements, positive visions, not-for-profit and helping initiatives, scientific and medical breakthroughs, heroic actions, collaborative and cooperative initiatives, moral/ethical decision making, and successful relationships. To showcase what's going right, writers and producers need only look for evidence of personal triumph or social improvement, including the many ways and opportunities to build body, mind, spirit, and enhance the quality of life of family, community, nation, and planet.

The Leading Edge

This series provides international coverage of leading-edge conferences, symposia, seminars, workshops, and expo's relating to personal growth and social development, those rich in fresh ideas and practical information. Programs would blend the best of speeches, panel discussions, interviews, events, book reviews, artistic expression, and entertaining performances.

Examples include: • International Congress of the World Future Society • World Health Congress • International Conference on Humor & Creativity • Association for Humanistic Psychology • International Conference on the Psychology of Health, Immunity and Disease • Infocomm International • Common Boundary Conference • National Whole Health Symposium & Expo • Global Forum Of Spiritual & Parliamentary Leaders • International Conferences of the Institute of Noetic Sciences • Body Mind Spirit Conference • Inner Idea Conference

Building Our Future

This magazine program reports on, advocates, and facilitates discussion about and development of the earth as a "sustainable garden paradise." The emphasis is on what people are doing to create a sustainable positive future for themselves, their families, companies, communities, and planet. News, information, profiles, feature stories, interviews, and exquisite imagery in a wide variety of fields combine to show what's being done and what can be done when we act as responsible stewards of the planet. In each program the hosts invite viewers to become involved in a variety of ways—where they live. Inspirational talks by authors and celebrities—voice-over beautiful imagery—contribute to the viewer's motivation to become involved.

Potentialist Turning-Points

This series profiles individuals who are realizing high levels of their potential. Each program presents the story of someone who had a turning-point realization that led them to commit to a goal that stretched their physical, mental, emotional, or spiritual capacities. Whatever the motivation, these people are on track to realize potentials beyond anything they could have expected. These stories inspire viewers to identify and realize their own potentials.

Books For Kids

This magazine program for children showcases everything to do with books—what's new, readings, signings, reviews, illustrations and illustrating, storytelling and story crafting, author profiles, creating books, and discussions facilitated by storytellers.

Producers of the various departments are located all across the country, producing their segments with kids in local bookstores. Some of the readings continue from week-to-week so kids look forward to the next episode. There are interactive games, opportunities for kids to text or email questions and comments. There would be a heavy reliance on visuals, music, and activities for the kids in their neighborhood bookstores. Sponsors would be obvious and abundant.

8

Content That Matters

We must now give equal time and focus, equal or even greater energy to those human qualities that are constructive, growth enhancing, confidence and trust inspiring, so that the power of these qualities can be consciously developed and applied both to individual lives and to the directing of societal and world affairs.

Janis A. Rose

IN CONSIDERING THE HIGHER POTENTIALS OF TELEVISION it must be emphasized that, whatever the content, its presentation must be either compelling or entertaining and produced with high production values. Otherwise people won't watch.

The bulleted programming concepts that follow the content descriptions below derive from the capacities cited in the previous chapter. Because they are merely sketches, they lack the context and essential presentational features—elaborated further on—that bring a program to life. Their purpose here is merely suggestive.

THE HIGHER CHARACTERISTICS OF HUMAN NATURE

Content for programming that matters flows naturally from the higher qualities and characteristics of human nature and consciousness. Subject matter is therefore considered *higher* relative to its contribution to our physical, mental, emotional, or spiritual health, also to the extent that it illuminates, demonstrates, or encourages the activation of higher human characteristics.

Acceptance	Contentment	Helpfulness	Positive
Aesthetics	Cooperation	Honesty	Respect
Altruism	Courage	Humility	Reverence
Appreciation	Creativity	Humor	Sharing
Awareness	Curiosity	Imagination	Spiritual
Awe	Discernment	Integrity	Insight
Beauty	Empathy	Intelligence	Tolerance
Caring	Faith	Intuition	Trust
Community	Flexibility	Kindness	Vision
Compassion	Forgiveness	Love	Wisdom
Confidence	Goodwill	Morality	Wonder
Connection	Gratitude	Patience	Zest for Life

A partial listing of higher human characteristics

When material on television activates or provides demonstrations of these characteristics, it succeeds in realizing the medium's higher potentials. An easy way to translate one of these characteristics into a programming concept is to specify the program's purpose as a verb to go with it. (Verbs are *italicized*. Virtues are in **bold**).

- This commercial will *associate* **intelligence** with (the product)
- This series of feature stories will *profile* **altruistic** initiatives in the area of...
- This documentary will *promote* an **appreciation** of...
- This newscast will *emphasize* the **positive** happenings in the community.
- This story *illustrates* the difference between passion and true **love**.
- These hour-long dramas will *demonstrate* **wisdom** in action.
- This series of PSA's will *increase* public **awareness** of…
- This television magazine will *include* ways for viewers to **connect**…

DESIRABLE (HEALTHY) VIEWER RESPONSES

Another approach to designing real-value programming is to identify the intended *outcome* for viewers. As a writer or producer, what do I want my audience to know, feel, appreciate, or otherwise take away from the experience of my program? What are the energies I want to feed into the social body?

A renowned television anchorman once said journalists couldn't be responsible for how viewers react to their stories. If by "responsible" he meant they cannot be held accountable for negative viewer responses such as committing suicide, copycat crimes, or domestic violence, he had a point. Indeed, a television station can output whatever it wants within the bounds of local decency standards without being held accountable for negative consequences.

Trouble is, we're beginning to realize the extent of our interdependence when it comes to mass communication. When messages from a nervous system consistently trigger startle responses and generate fear, that energy ripples throughout the body. If it builds up due to repetition, the body builds defenses and becomes rigid. Prolonged, this can result in a general malaise, feelings of helplessness, anger, and depression.

While the First Amendment allows open and free communication, writers, journalists, and producers who understand the extent of our interconnectedness—and that what we express into the world we make more of—will actually *want* to assume responsibility for the energies they feed into the social body. Preferring to contribute to the health, well-being, and vitality of their viewers—by extension the community—they will want their offerings to be nutritional.

Vaclav Havel (Past-president of Czechoslovakia):

> "Those who have the mass media in their hands bear responsibility for the world, for the future of humanity. Just as splitting the atom can immensely enrich humanity in a thousand and one ways and at the same time threaten it with destruction, so television can have both good and evil consequences. Quickly, suggestively, and to an unprecedented degree, it can disseminate the spirit of understanding, humanity, human solidarity, and spirituality, or it can stupefy whole nations and continents."

I worked for two affiliated television stations and a PBS station, beginning as a cinematographer and moving into the roles of Director of Photography (DP), writer, and producer. In each of these situations, I and my colleagues were so focused on our productions—commercials, documentaries, and special projects—we gave little to no thought to the needs of the audience, much less what effect our work would have on them. Because production decisions were based on either the needs of advertisers or the current interests of the stations' owners and managers, all we cared about was making our presentations compelling or entertaining.

By sitting with family members and watching together the commercials and programs I'd produced, I began to notice that, although they were pleased with my work, there were instances when the subject matter and how we handled it elicited emotional responses I hadn't anticipated.

The first instance of this was when I was called down to the newsroom to fill in for photographers who were all out on assignment. As a producer of commercials and documentaries who'd never shot news footage before, I asked the news director what he wanted in the way of coverage. The police scanner reported a pileup on the Interstate and all he cared about was getting a camera on the scene fast. There was no time for instruction.

When I arrived on the scene, three wrecked cars were scattered across highway. Cop cars had their colored lights flashing and traffic was being re-routed. A man laying in the street was being treated by paramedics. I got wide and medium shots from several angles. Closer in, I pointed the camera wherever I saw something dramatic: The injured man holding his head, paramedics running with medical kits, the wrecked cars, a woman sitting by the side of the road crying with red lights flashing across her face.

The news director expressed his gratitude and appreciation as I handed off the film for processing and editing. Watching the finished story on the eleven o'clock newscast made me sick. I'd provided the editor with everything he needed to ramp up the drama. There hadn't been any serious injuries. What viewers saw looked more like a scene from a hospital drama. The woman appeared to be crying for the man whose head was being attended to, but she didn't even know the injured man. In retrospect, the story should have at least in part been about the way the police, fire, and medical professionals had handled the situation. Instead of giving viewers pride and hope, we elicited sympathy and contributed to feelings of vulnerability.

In the months and years that followed, there were other instances where I was less than proud of my role as producer. The curious thing is that nobody ever told us to sensationalize, exaggerate, or misrepresent, but that's what we were doing, particularly in our commercials. The medium itself creates an expectation that's easy to go along with, especially for creative people eager to exercise their ability to move people.

Years later, when my research into the higher capacities of television was well underway and I was producing real-value programming, I looked back and realized that I wouldn't have had to leave my job in order to produce with awareness and integrity. I could have argued alternative production approaches with supervisors. I could have chosen projects more carefully. I could have chosen different people to work with. I could have incorporated more substance, less sensationalism and fluff in my productions. Especially, I could have taken into consideration the *effect* my productions would have on viewers. That alone would have made my early productions more of a contribution—and given me more satisfaction.

Awareness	Encouragement	Joy
Awe	Engagement	Motivation
Compassion	Enhancement	Optimism
Commitment	Enrichment	Pride
Determination	Enthusiasm	Resolution
Diligence	Expanded POV	Self-confidence
Discipline	Humor	Sensitivity
Education	Inspiration	Understanding
Empowerment	Interest	Upliftment

A partial listing of positive, health-promoting viewer outcomes

For your next project, select a desirable audience outcome that you as writer or producer want your audience to know or feel, and then express it as a verb in the program's purpose statement. Notice in the examples below that the verb and the outcome are the same. If you accomplish one, you accomplish the other.

- The purpose of this commercial is to *encourage* viewers to…
- The purpose of this program is to *inspire* audiences to…
- This series is intended to *empower* young women to…
- These stories must *educate* people on the importance of…
- This program will *enhance* the community's appreciation for...

9

Socially Responsible Programming

This instrument can teach, it can illuminate; yes, and it can even inspire. But it can do so only to the extent that humans are determined to use it to those ends. Otherwise it is merely wires and lights in a box.

Edward R. Murrow

SPECIFICALLY, WHAT CAN TELEVISION DO IN THE AREA OF *programming* to facilitate health and well-being, and help viewers adjust to change appropriately? What kinds of programs have nutritional (real) value? How can those who make and shape programming content make television that's more than "wires and lights in a box?"

SHOWCASE ACCOMPLISHMENT

Especially important for a social body are programs that present the successes and accomplishments of its members, including demonstrations of excellence. A human nervous system that only processes threats and breakdowns runs the risk of convincing the whole body that dysfunction is normal.

Besides dealing with trouble, a responsible nervous system encourages its members to move in the direction of balance, cohesion, and harmony. One of the reasons why sports are so popular as both activity and entertainment is that they present challenges which, when met, are opportunities to celebrate. Whether in sports or any other activity, meeting challenges and celebrating accomplishment teaches us lessons, stimulates hope for the future, demonstrates that transcendence is possible, and shows us that dreams can and do come true.

Bruce Lipton (Biologist):

> "Individual success depends on environments that trigger the fulfillment of our genetic potential. Environments that motivate through fear literally shut down the potential for growth. Those that motivate through vision, open us up to express unforeseen possibilities."

- Profiles of excellence in every field, focusing on process and intrinsic rewards
- The spirit of volunteerism, cooperation, and service
- Celebrations of completion: a skyscraper, a ship, a long journey, business goals
- Personal transformation: overcoming obesity, addiction, abusive relationships, physical limitations
- The realization of seemingly impossible goals or dreams
- Models of people living less from expectations and more from authentic purpose, values, and vision
- Profiles of successful high-performing or synergistic teams
- New technologies and research results that change the way we live and work

DEMONSTRATE AND ENCOURAGE CREATIVE DEVELOPMENT AND EXPRESSION

After a lifetime of studying the rise and fall of civilizations, Arnold Toynbee said one of the hallmarks of great civilizations was the encouragement, support, and celebration of the artists who made the society's values, ideals, and ideas more tangible, more assessable to the general population.

Aesthetic experience and expression transforms the ordinary and mundane into the special and meaningful. It refines the personality and enriches the soul. Since there seem to be few opportunities for everyday people to engage their aesthetic potentials unless their career demands it, television could help us tap into it by introducing people in all walks of life who are expressing their creativity in ways that are intelligent, constructive, meaningful, and inspiring. Programs that spotlight the creative process and encourage aesthetic appreciation and experience would inspire and enable more people to manifest beauty, order, and meaning in their lives and in the world. For those not inclined to exercise their creativity, seeing others so engaged would at least contribute to their understanding of and appreciation for those who are.

- Profiles of artists who can demonstrate and articulate their aesthetic quest
- Instruction on the aesthetic dimensions: form, line, contrast, gradation...
- Interviews to understand artists' experience of beauty, harmony, order
- Examination of the qualities in creative works that uplift and inspire
- Documentary on artistic responses to nature across cultures
- Profiles of talented unknown or little-known artists and their works
- Examination of values pertaining to art: Fame. Expression. Profit.
- A "How to" series that teaches and inspires the use of fine art materials
- Profiles of local and national art exhibitions narrated by celebrities
- Parenting that encourages creative potentials to be more fully expressed

MEANINGFULLY CONNECT US AND ILLUMINATE OUR INTERDEPENDENCE

Meaningful connection facilitates mutually beneficial relationships including healthy perspectives of and beyond us. It helps us position ourselves personally, professionally, and spiritually so we can play our part and live more fulfilled and conscious lives. As long as we see ourselves as separate from nature, one another and other cultures, as long as we consider human nature to be fundamentally flawed, we will continue to sully, exploit, and ignore our larger social bodies and ecosystems without much guilt.

But when we realize that our planetary body is both home and a magnificent living presence in the cosmos, when we see its immensity and grandeur, the complexity and beauty of its interconnected ecosystems and realize that it's a single, self-renewing, self-knowing, living, and evolving system with many and diverse cultural members dependent upon its physical body for survival, we can never again abuse or ignore it.

Elisabet Sahtouris (Evolutionary biologist, business consultant):

> "Living things have to change in order to stay the same; they have to renew themselves and to adjust to the changes around them. Rabbits evolve together in their 'rabbitats,' all creatures evolve in connection with all else evolving around them."

Connection to Higher Self

- Programs that profile masters adept at listening to the "still small voice within"
- A series featuring motivational speakers set in shopping malls across the country so everyday people can comment and ask questions
- A series of visually stimulating, guided meditations presented by leading experts in the art of awareness
- Instruction and exercise in techniques such as yoga, tai chi, chi gong and other integrating body-mind exercises
- Profiles of individuals and communities from the full spectrum of spiritual traditions, all responding to the same set of meaningful questions
- Instruction and demonstration on the use of assessment tools to help viewers identify their unique gifts, governing values, vocation of destiny...
- Strategies for getting onto the path of true vocation, beyond occupation or social expectation
- Processes for envisioning and living, as Oprah puts it, "our best life."
- Master-student dialogues on spiritual growth and development

Connection to Resources

A series that matches needs and resources—

- Profiles of individuals and families that have "fallen through the cracks" and need a boost
- Scholars looking for researchers, assistants, data-entry support
- Connecting parents with resources to better home-school their children
- Artists looking for materials; musicians putting together a band
- Community resources bulletin board
- Connecting prospective employees with potential employers
- Profiles of law firms and their specialties
- Profiles of community nonprofit organizations and their services
- Profiles of global helping organizations: NGO's)
- Profiles of local and national environmental organizations and resources

- Information and profiles of city-wide recycling initiatives, stations, and support
- On location profiles of venues where there are opportunities to volunteer and help locally, nationally, and internationally

Connection to Diverse Cultures (Promoting understanding and tolerance)

- Anthropologists who show and explain various cultures' relationship beliefs and rituals; what they contribute to individuals and the culture
- Samplings of world-views across cultures
- Examination of the social-cultural mechanisms that contribute to warfare and peace
- How a culture's creation stories influence everyday living
- Tracing genetic lines of various cultures from the present to the distant past
- Examining the structures of language and how they contribute to ethnic identity
- Profiles of primitive religions; the nature and significance of belief

Connection to the Science and Beauty of the Natural World and Cosmos

- Evolutionary science brought up to date
- The many physical ways in which we are interconnected and interdependent
- Evidence of order: fractal geometry, quantum physics, sacred geometry
- Inspiring montages of landscapes and seascapes, ecosystems, animals, plants
- The wonders of the universe beyond the earth
- Life processes and living systems; the nature of order, chaos, and complexity
- One day road trips to experience nature (locally and nationally)
- Inspiring lectures by the great scientists of our time
- Aerial and satellite images of the earth set to music
- Science in your own household, backyard, and neighborhood

CELEBRATE AND PROMOTE DIVERSITY

Television has embraced ethnic and gender diversity, but it has yet to show in any consistent manner *that* and *how* our differences, when respected and integrated, promote social cohesion and long term resilience. Diversity is nature's way of insuring that *variety* and *flexibility*, essential components of the evolutionary process, are optimized to meet the challenges of change.

The prime example, of course, is the United States of America. It's no accident that the most powerful and wealthiest nation in human history began as a melting pot. Just as steel is made stronger by the introduction of carbon and other diverse elements, just as cell immunity is enhanced by increased molecular diversity, just as an ecosystem is vitalized by diverse species, so a society is made stronger by the interaction of diverse individuals.

Our television screens have been saturated with evidence of diversity's ability to divide and enflame, but they can also provide evidence of its potential to unify and strengthen, show us what's possible when people of different ethnic backgrounds, belief systems, status, and sexual orientation compliment each other when they join hearts and hands to achieve mutually beneficial goals. Despite television's propensity to create drama (audience share) by fanning the flames of cultural or political differences, its greater power and higher potential will be realized in its ability to inspire, mediate, and facilitate.

David Gerzon (Social engineer):

> "Diversity, though hard to encompass in our fixed ideologies, may turn out in the end to be the key to our survival."

- Diverse people collaborating to realize common, mutually beneficial goals
- Diverse people engaging in respectful and reasoned discourse
- Face-to-face formal dialogues on community challenges that generate positive solutions
- Profiles of diverse lifestyles to show that we have more in common than in difference
- Examples to show that former enemies can become friends when they listen and come to understand each other, particularly their life stories
- How a passion for realizing common goals can break down the walls of division and animosity
- The nature of stereotypes; how they emerge and are perpetuated
- Model schools or corporations where diversity has become a prime asset
- Profiles of diverse and successful leaders in all sectors
- Examination of the dynamic and causal relationships between diversity and poverty—and what can be done about it

ACTIVATE EMPATHY

As noted, a social body cannot tolerate a nervous system that only awakens its members to their needs when disasters strike. There needs to be early detection in order to reduce the likelihood or seriousness of a potential crisis. Prevention measures need to be in place. And these can be derived through the assimilation of lessons learned from previous breakdowns. There's great wisdom in the adage: If the lessons of the past are not learned, they're bound to be repeated.

Another discovery made by Arnold Toynbee was that the level of *maturity* of a civilization and the *duration* of its viability is best indicated by the way the people at the top of the society responded to the needs of the people at the bottom. Television has a successful track record of hosting telethons and appeals, particularly in response to national and natural disasters, but much more can be done to respond to the needs of everyday people who, for whatever reason, are disadvantaged. When television shows us people in need or suffering, it is natural for viewers to want to help. Through programs that activate empathy close to home and regularly, our children and we would learn how best to assist close at home and where help is needed most.

Kahlil Gibran (Artist, poet, author):

> "Tenderness and kindness are not signs of weakness and despair, but manifestations of strength and resolution."

- Models of success in the areas of homelessness, begging, domestic abuse, drug-related crime
- Anonymous matching of the needs of disadvantaged people with people and resources that can help
- Profiles of local organizations that need volunteers or support; how viewers can participate
- Profiles of people in need (personalizing provides insight and diffuses stereotypes)
- Profiles of community facilities and the services they offer
- Family makeovers: collaborative initiatives to give needy families a boost or fresh start
- Cooperative efforts to assist people—to the extent possible—in life-threatening situations
- Rescues of people who have gotten themselves into difficult circumstances

- Profiles that demonstrate the effectiveness of counseling, re-training, and various therapies
- Local documentary series that reports on poverty and calls viewers to participate in solutions

FACILITATE CIVIC AND SOCIAL ENGAGEMENT

Consistent with the activation function of a nervous system, Webster's New Collegiate Dictionary describes the term *mediator as* "an intermediary agent," one who stands in the middle. As a mass communications medium, television stands in the middle between the individual viewer and the social body. It's place is not on the sidelines overseeing those embroiled in action—as if to observe is not to influence what is being observed—but in the middle of things where the issues, ideas, ideologies, and events clash, twist, mix and become resolved.

As an intermediary agent, a television network, channel, or station can insure that the process of engagement goes well, that key perspectives are represented, that participants are respectful, that everyone has equal opportunity to contribute, that the facts are accurate and available to all, that the interaction is focused, and that reasonable options and solutions are explored.

Despite criticism from journalists who think the media's place is on the sidelines, that objectivity is possible, and that their primary role is as political watchdog, experience in many communities has shown that when the media engage the public, everyone wins. Democracy works best when an informed public becomes engaged.

Davis (Buzz) Merritt (Journalist):

> "Without active public engagement in the issues of the day, which is to say without viable agoras (information venues), democracy cannot function properly. Where such discussions and engagements are not occurring, journalists have a responsibility to help it occur."

- Editorial comments presented by everyday citizens
- Models of formal (intelligent, respectful, and productive) dialogue
- Citizen groups imagine optimal civic performance: excellence in police work, the judicial system, waste collection, infrastructure maintenance

- The lessons we should be learning from patterns in the local news
- Models of the tools, techniques, and processes of conflict resolution
- A think-tank where solutions to community challenges are envisioned by experts and citizens
- A program that asks citizens to offer their vision of their most desirable community
- Documentation of civic processes: local elections, courts, police, utilities, local governance
- Clear definition of opposing perspectives: Republican/Democrat, Free/Fair Trade, Pro-life/Pro-choice, Big/small government, socialism/capitalism
- What democracy looks like when it's approached as a verb rather than a noun

SHOW US THE BIG PICTURE

What's going on in the holons above us? Local news may be more relevant than international news, but that doesn't mean we have no interest in the lives of people beyond our cities, nation, and region. The more clearly we can see and understand the nature of family, organization, society, nation, planet, cosmos—how they function well and how they integrate—the better we'll be able to find the appropriate fit between our personal stories and the larger entities within which we function. Programming that would situate the individual within these larger wholes would contribute substantially to individual identity, purpose, direction, and meaning—and improve relationships.

Brian Swimme (Cosmologist) and Thomas Berry (Ecologist):

> "There is eventually only one story, the story of the universe. Every form of being is integral with this comprehensive story. Nothing is itself without everything else."

- Global warming challenges and appropriate responses from the perspective of multi-cultural scientists
- Health, health delivery systems, breakdowns and breakthroughs around the world
- Outcomes of global research that can improve the quality of life locally and globally
- Successes in social experiments: family, commerce, religion, business

- Global treasures: libraries, museums, churches, monasteries, mosques, synagogues show us the treasures we'd otherwise never see
- Sacred sites: nature, study, history, use, research
- Artistic trends and movements in the fine arts around the world
- Endangered species and environments: status, challenges, possible solutions, what we can do
- Global education: where it's working; great schools, great teachers
- Great minds: cosmologists, physicists, biologists, ecologists, mathematicians present the sum and substance of their work; theories, predictions

SHARE THE BEST IN US WITH THE REST OF US

The best in us is made visible through demonstrations of our higher characteristics, virtues such as altruism, service, dedication, volunteerism, cooperation, discipline, intelligent creativity, healing, sacrifice, sharing, helping, and heroism. Western capitalism inclines us toward criticism, cynicism, and materialism, modes of thinking which can smother appreciation, optimism, and aesthetic appreciation. To counteract these tendencies we need to see that people are good, that virtuous behavior is also part of human nature, that there's more to life than commerce, violence, sexuality, and glamour, that we have within us all that's necessary to resolve our differences, solve our problems, and transcend the limitations of narrow, self-centered and consumption-oriented thinking which is bringing us down and despoiling the planet.

Ralph Waldo Emerson (Essayist, lecturer, poet):

> "What lies behind us and what lies before us are tiny matters compared to what lies within us."

- Everyday people, even children, making a difference in their community
- Profiles of courage, caring, integrity, altruism, entrepreneurship, humanitarianism
- Profiles of people and families who are well-adjusted and living happy, full, and fulfilled lives
- Couples who have found true and lasting love
- Thriving intentional communities

- Authors and poets who write for the joy of writing (rather than getting published)
- Athletes whose spirit and strength of character match the strength of their bodies
- Teachers of all ages and at all levels who inspire and empower their students
- Servant-leaders in business and government

ENRICH OUR LIVES

For microbiologists an "enrichment medium" is any environment that promotes the growth of a particular organism by providing it with essential nutrients. Just so, a television enterprise can become a source of enrichment by providing its viewers with nutrients—information and images that make life healthier, happier, fuller, more meaningful, productive, or fulfilling. Nutritional programs promote overall health, stimulate our minds, feed our souls, and strengthen our connections to others, the world, and the cosmos. They enrich our lives.

Lyndon B. Johnson (Past President):

> "The Great Society is a place where every child can find knowledge to enrich his mind and to enlarge his talents. It is a place where the city of man serves not only the needs of the body and the demands of commerce but the desire for beauty and the hunger for community. It is a place where men are more concerned with the quality of their goals than the quantity of their goods."

- A television magazine that focuses on the positive happenings of the day
- Mini-dramas of historical figures who exemplified qualities of character
- Evolutionary biologists illustrate the dynamics of the evolutionary process
- Using stunning imagery, an ecologist tells how ecosystems are sustained
- Earth commercials that make it "cool" to respect the natural world
- Everyday people articulate their dreams for their families and community
- Scholars and scientists present reasons to be optimistic about the future
- Stories of remission from terminal illness

EXPOSE US TO WHOLE-SYSTEM PRINCIPLES AND THEIR PRACTICAL APPLICATIONS

The models we inherited with regard to how the world works are no longer viable. If humanity is to meet the demands of the future, personally and socially, there needs to be a shift away from the "subdue the earth," mechanical model of the universe which says it's fixed, determined, inert, and knowable, to an understanding that the universe is one, whole, open, self-making, interconnected system that's permeated with living qualities, if not life itself. Television programs can educate us in this regard, and they can encourage us to relate to each other and the planet in ways that are more respectful, fulfilling, and sustainable.

Richard C. Dorf (Professor of Engineering & Systems Science):

> "From a systems design perspective, the global capitalist economy is well suited to the task of rapidly exploiting natural and human resources for the purpose of inflating the financial assets of a small elite. It is ill suited to the task of creating a just, sustainable, and compassionate society that works for all on a finite living planet."

- An entertaining series that presents whole-systems sciences for lay people, updating what's being taught in high schools and colleges
- A comedy show that presents satirical skits that illustrate right-relationship: person to person, employee to employer, young to elderly, gay to straight, spouse to spouse, citizen to government, person to planet
- A documentary series on the local infrastructure: background, design, maintenance, improved technologies, costs and who pays for it
- A documentary series on how local, state, and federal systems operate
- A "How to" home maintenance series that approaches houses as whole-systems, demonstrating what needs to be done in order to stave off entropy
- Documentaries on the city's water processing and energy producing systems
- Nation wide models of effective waste and recycling programs

FACILITATE FEEDBACK

Individual and collective living systems require constant and accurate performance information from their component members in order to know what's working and what's not working. The internet allows us to send messages to anyone, anywhere, immediately and at little cost, so it has become the preferred medium for facilitating the exchange of feedback information.

Nonetheless, television can play a key role in this area by virtue of it being a *shared* rather than *private* experience. A variety of media guides and some inserts in television news provide feedback relating to the consumption of goods and a smattering of services. But there is little to no feedback on how well or how poorly civic, social, and governmental institutions, processes, and services are performing. A program that would provide accurate information about these would go a long toward increasing understanding, reducing waste, redundancy, and corruption, and helping citizens to make better decisions when it comes to money management and voting.

Norbert Wiener (System's scientist, originator of cybernetics):

> "Feedback is a method of controlling a system by reinserting into it the results of past performance...if feedback can change the pattern of performance, then we have a process which may very well be called learning."

- Periodic performance "report cards" on entitlement programs; cost/benefit analysis
- Performance "report cards" for local governmental agencies and nonprofit organizations
- Annual awards banquet & program: local initiatives that contributed most to the community
- Citizen reviews of best/worse city services; how the worst can improve
- Annual review of local priorities; how they have been met/not met; what needs to be done
- Comedy skits that satirize local politicians and their perspectives on issues
- Awards program for corporate entities that have done the most to improve the community
- Instruction and guidance on how to provide feedback that will be heard and taken seriously

- Open forum or formal dialogues where everyday citizens connect with city managers
- Documentary on the city's budgetary allotments and rationales in plain and uncomplicated language with graphic animation

CONNECT US TO THE GLOBAL FAMILY

Local and national electronic nervous systems do only part of their job if they don't also provide information and images that reference the full spectrum of human diversity and experience. What's more, reporting on other cultures and nations only when they're experiencing trauma is not responsible with respect to the planetary body.

The ideal would be for all members of the global body to have continuous and accurate information about all the other members, but that's a long way off. For now, the electronic nervous systems that have global information gathering capability could and should be improving our picture of the humanity and the human condition beyond wars, disasters, cuisines, and vacation spots.

It's nearly impossible to watch television news and not see how deeply interrelated we are. Disturbances in one nation ripple influences throughout the others overnight. Globally, what farmers grow and how they grow it, what manufacturers make and how they make it, what politicians decide and don't decide, carry consequences for the entire human family. The more cultural diversity we can experience, respect, and incorporate, the better prepared we'll be as a species to respond to whole-systems challenges.

Beatrice Bruteau (Philosopher and author):

> "We are being drawn into a partnership, a connective network with all our neighbors, that is run by, and even centrally consists of, communication. It resembles nothing so much as a huge conversation, a planetary conversation."

- A program that samples the perspectives of people in other cultures to see how they view the issues that most concern everyday Americans
- Profiles of people and initiatives that are making a positive difference in the countries closest to us (Mexico, Central America, Canada)
- A series of programs that present the unique attributes, resources, and contributions that various nations are making to the global body
- Profiles of various nations' national treasures—exemplary citizens

- Around the world: governmental policies & practices that are improving the lives of everyday citizens
- On location stories that profile opportunities to work or volunteer abroad
- Coverage of international conferences, exhibitions, and national celebrations
- Examination of various cultures' manners, customs, rituals, and protocols in business, the arts, sports, and entertainment
- Documentary series: What are the social concerns uppermost in the minds of people in various nations? And what is their response?

PROVIDE ACCESS TO THE GREAT MINDS AND SOULS OF OUR TIME

Conventional television offerings provide a great deal of information to help us develop our physical being, but is practically silent when it comes to developing our mental, emotional, and spiritual aspects. Just as it presents models of healthy bodies, it can also provide models of our other endowments by providing regular, shared, and ideally interactive access to the great minds and souls of our time.

I would characterize "great minds" as individuals who have acquired knowledge, insight, and understanding by focusing on matters of significance, meaning, value, and possibility. As a result, these people sometimes make exceptional observations and connections, and thereby challenge the rest of us to see or think in new or expanded ways. Whereas their minds are stimulated and enriched by knowledge that comes from exposure to other thinkers, the core of their insight and understanding more often bubbles up from within.

"Great souls" are people whose obvious goodness is matched with qualities such as openness, wisdom, humility, and good humor. In their personality expression they demonstrate kindness and a refinement of character. Their orientation is often toward service to others, and they are committed to truth as far as they can understand it. If they have a spiritual teacher or guru, they make a good faith effort to represent the beloved's consciousness and spirit in their everyday lives.

Rabbi Michael Lerner (Progressive activist and publisher):

> "Were we to understand our fundamental interconnections, we would recognize that our own well-being or the development of our soul and consciousness is totally dependent on the development of every other human being on the planet."

SHOWCASE AND ENCOURAGE INNOVATION

In order to adjust to change appropriately, individuals and social bodies need information about their options, especially those that provide models for new or improved ways of being and doing. Evolution is nature's way of continuously discovering and building upon improvements. *Newness* is a lateral advance, an improvement in a current situation or system, as when an automobile manufacturer produces a new model; it mainly affects same-level holons. Drivers. *Radical newness* occurs when the advancement is vertical, the bringing about of a form or function that affects the holons above and below it. System-wide change is a radical improvement, for instance a car that runs on hydrogen or sunlight. Newness results in *historical* change. Radical newness results in *evolutionary* change, which requires circumstances and environments where creative individuals have the time and opportunity to imagine and play. Radical newness also requires a free and fertile exchange of ideas, a place where wonder is allowed free range and the resources are available to try and fail without the pressures of deadlines, budget constraints, or the need to turn a profit. That's why it's so rare.

It's also why evolutionary innovation comes more from individuals and small teams than corporations. Thomas Edison, Henry Ford, George Eastman, Bill Gates and Steve Jobs created innovations on their own or with the help of a friend. Nobody did a market study to determine if the public wanted a horseless carriage, a machine for talking across long distances, a box that would capture images and put them on paper, a picture tube that could capture live motion and sounds, the personal computer, or even tissues to blow one's nose into rather than a handkerchief.

In addition to the utility that derives from them, innovations of all kinds provide evidence that imagination, ingenuity, perseverance, and intelligent creativity are active in the world. And that gives us hope. If television could show us the innovators of our day, in and across all spheres of interest, more of us would be inspired to consider improvements and options in our own areas of interest.

Anonymous:

"You don't make history by doing what's already been done."

- A series of programs that profile innovators and their evolutionary innovations, including those under development

- A situation room that maps and connects technical and social innovations globally
- Profiles of innovations in the area of ecosystem sustainability
- Rapid response innovations to global crises such as hurricane Katrina, 9/11, the Haiti hurricane, and the Japanese tsunamis and earthquakes
- Social innovations that are proving their worth in health, education, early childhood development, elder care, community building
- Innovations in business (manufacturing, sales, marketing, R&D, human capital, partnerships)
- Educating for innovation; how to encourage and foster imagination, wonder, and exploration in children and adults
- Public invitational: Hosts invite viewers to present their innovations and ideas
- Worldwide profiles of *companies* where fostering innovation is a priority

SHOWCASE THE PUBLIC WISDOM

Since one of the higher functions of television is to contribute to personal growth and social development, one of the most direct ways to accomplish this is to provide access to people who best illuminate the higher reaches of human nature and experience. When journalists, narrators, actors, and other presenters are wearing their professional hats, they are *secondary* representatives of the human condition. They highlight, describe or interpret the lives of *other* people. For them to be *primary* representatives, the stories they tell would have to be about *themselves*. Primary sources are first-hand experiencers, those who tell their own story. These are the folks in the know and in the middle, thoughtful and caring people who have gained wisdom and insight through life experience.

These people can teach us about the art of living, by example. Where and how did they grow up? What were the key events and turning points in their lives? What were their primary influences? Motives? Trials? Inspirations? Challenges? How did they respond to life-crises? What were the lessons learned?

Television can be candid and personal, spontaneous, rather than formal and politically correct. As life speeds up and the use of electronic devices results in less face-to-face interaction, the meanings that ordinarily derive from contact with people other than those closest to us, are being narrowed. Access to the insights and perspectives of people we *don't* know helps us affirm and modify our own view of life and living. It's how we come to share a common identity as a people, and construct our personal realities. Also, it's one of the best ways to develop an appreciation for human diversity. Among other things, getting into the minds, hearts, souls, and experiences of others helps us refine our sense of self and encompass more of the world beyond us. So who are these everyday purveyors of public wisdom?

Silvia Boorstein (Psychotherapist, storyteller):

> "You can't see wisdom, but you can see its reflection. Its reflection is happiness, fearlessness, and kindness."

- Profiles of people who have endured adversity, trauma, repression, or abuse
- People who have maintained deep and healthy relationships and marriages
- People who can make connections between the past and present
- Individuals on a quest of personal transformation
- Unconventional thinkers, doers, and problem-solvers
- Politicians who listen, who seek to discover rather than proclaim
- Scientists who can communicate their work in simple, everyday language
- Healers of all stripes who are consistently effective
- Parents who are succeeding at parenting
- Social activists who understand how to affect *graceful* positive change

SHOWCASE VISIONARIES AND THEIR VISIONS

Every tool and technology that has ever been invented, every building, social structure, cultural meme, fashion, and lifestyle exists as it does today because someone envisioned them that way. Discontent pushes us away from what is, and the desire for something better compels us to dream of options and possibilities. Because envisioning the future plants the seeds for tomorrow's realities, television should be showcasing people who are far seers. Dreamers. Visionaries. According to social engineer, Willis Harman, "Affirming a positive vision may be about the most sophisticated action any one of us can take."

Who are these visionaries? Where do we find them? Only rarely are they celebrities. More often they carry titles such as *entrepreneur, architect, scientist, activist, author, city planner, CEO, artist, engineer, teacher, philosopher, healer, ecologist, technologist, futurist*. They're people who, for whatever reason, have developed an expanded vision in their area of interest. They are like us in that they're not satisfied with the way things are. But unlike us they find ways to dream the possible and make it come true. While the rest of us are keeping the boat afloat and rowing toward the dock, these people are looking beyond to distant shores, as if through high-powered telescopes. Perhaps their most distinguishing characteristic is a passion that transcends the traditional payoffs of money, status, fame, glamour, or ambition. Even the desire to make a difference. They want a different reality. They want to live their dream—more expansive ways of being, more satisfying ways of working, more harmonious social orders, new political contexts, healthy and sustainable environments, new paradigms, new worlds, and new definitions of what it means to be human. Now, anything they can dream can be realized on the screen.

Programming that would provide access to visionaries and their visions would help viewers find increased enthusiasm for using our own imaginations constructively.

Proverbs, XXIX:

"Where there is no vision, the people perish."

- Visually stimulating programs of visionaries presenting their visions—
    - Of social harmony
    - Of advanced communication technologies
    - Of planned communities
    - Of architecture
    - Of space exploration and travel
    - Of modes of transportation
    - Of more effective and profitable manufacturing processes
    - Of sustainability
    - Of innovation in education

SHOW US HOW THE WORLD WORKS

For young people and many adults, knowing something about the social systems within which they live and work can help them find their place in the world and provide advantages. Although 84% of Americans graduate from high school, most have not been exposed to the financial workings or operating systems of the larger holons wherein they will spend their lives (U.S. Census Bureau, 2011). Models for jobs and careers come mainly from family, relatives, and friends—

and television that glamorizes a very narrow spectrum of options. Lacking, is exposure to the full spectrum of occupational models, particularly knowledge of the principles and practices of the systems that provide livelihood and fuel the economy.

At a very practical level, systemic principles and subjects such as information theory, chaos and complexity theory, interpersonal communication, energy and information exchange, and synergy would be especially appropriate subjects for television because knowledge in these areas contributes to success across the board in relationships and jobs.

Consider the prospect of a team of television writers and producers taking on the challenge of creating entertaining programs that model higher human characteristics in the full spectrum of workplace environments where the characters encounter *real* challenges (as opposed to the life and death dramas of cop and hospital shows). Life is the ultimate drama, not death or the threat of it. Although the examples below suggest non-fictional approaches, each of these environments is rich with opportunities for fictional approaches as well.

Margaret Wheatley (Management and systems consultant):

"Life is intent on finding what works, not what's right."

- **Financial systems***:* (Considering the audience only has a high school education) What's involved in getting a loan? How do banks make money? Where and how can stocks, bonds, and other securities be purchased? What are the different ways to save and invest? What constitutes wise investment?
- **Corporate systems**: What are the implications of different corporate structures? How does one prepare for and then secure a job or begin a career track in a corporate environment? What are the positions and salary ranges at various levels? What are the associated lifestyles? What constitutes a good fit between employer and employee?
- **Local government***:* What are the different offices and services? How do the various systems work: water and sewage, waste collection and recycling, the post office, taxes, zoning laws, courts, penal system. How does one prepare for and secure employment in the government sector? What is the pay scale? Advancement? Lifestyle?
- **Federal government***:* Structure, interrelationships, departments, operations, jobs and career tracks?

- **Service systems**: Hospitals, fire and rescue operations, food banks, homeless shelters, social services, United Way, nursing homes, government sponsored volunteer services such as the Peace Corps and the Corporation For National Service.
- **Academic systems:** How do they work? How does one apply for college? What does it take to get accepted? Loans and financial aid. Communication protocols. What are classes like at different universities? Departments and degree requirements. Scholarships. Academic status and hierarchies. Job prospects. The tenure process: reasoning, implications, and benefits.
- **Ecosystems**: How do they work, bottom to top? Management? Jobs and lifestyles in ecosystem management.
- **Religious systems**: How are they structured? How do they operate? What do they offer? Models of engagement. Lifestyles.

MODELS OF PERSONAL TRANSFORMATION

Programming in this area needs no elaboration beyond citing the prime example, *The Oprah Winfrey Show*, which brilliantly showcased her journey from poverty to riches, obscurity to celebrity, tragedy to triumph. The long-running program demonstrated conclusively that well-produced, mindful television—in this case the overarching theme of personal transformation—can be compelling and entertaining. The sustained and enormous success of the program is an indication of the public's hunger for television that matters.

James O'Dea (Former director of Amnesty International):
"Transformation is the process that facilitates the movement from limiting and constricting forms of identification to something larger, more inclusive, and more whole."

DOING GOOD WHILE ENTERTAINING

Along with *The Oprah Winfrey Show*, ABC's *Extreme Makeover: Home Edition* is another prime example of a program that entertains while doing good. The formula is simple: Find a human challenge or need, pull together resources such as commercial sponsors, local businesses, and neighbors to fulfill it, record it on video, and package it with a charismatic presenter and high production values.

Of course this takes money and talent, but these programs deliver *long-term* and *multiple* returns on investment: profitability, high levels of public relations and good will for the network and sponsors, and community development to name a few. Doing good while entertaining is a field that can be substantially widened, locally and internationally.

Abraham Maslow (Developmental psychologist):

> "That society is good which fosters the fullest development of human potentials, the fullest degree of humanness."

- A "reality" series that pays full-ride college tuition, fees, and boarding for high-potential individuals who otherwise could never afford to go to college
- A series that rebuilds an entire street or community in an area devastated by natural disaster
- A series that calls out an entire community to plant trees in a burned forest.
- Pay all medical expenses for an individual denied or lacking health care insurance through no fault of their own.
- Fulfill the dreams of talented people by assigning them celebrity mentors.
- Secure jobs for qualified people living on the edge.
- Upgrade nursing home facilities with appropriate equipment, furnishings, and technologies.
- Provide materials and motivation for citizens to clean-up, paint-up, and beautify their homes and community.
- Provide after-school self-defense training for elementary and high-school students who live in depressed neighborhoods.
- Provide skill development for people out of work because the skills they had are no longer marketable.

Part VI

Program Development

10

The Changing Demand

Television has an obligation to do more than entertain.
Richard H. Frank

TELEVISION PROFESSIONALS WILL UNDERSTANDABLY ASK: Why should we create this kind of programming when the public is content and we're already making a profit? Why spend money when we don't have to? Why set programming goals that are challenging or risky when it's not necessary? Why blaze a trail up hill when the tour busses covering the valley are popular and making money? Why should a company venture into the mountains where the roads are poorly paved and the air rarified, especially since it costs more to get there and the number of travelers is likely to be fewer?

Simply put, because that's where the peaks are! Life is an ascent. And although television has not yet discovered it, that's where the demand of the future is being shaped. In fact, the demand is already there. Educated and aging Americans, segments of the population that are growing rapidly, have either arrived at or are venturing toward the peaks. Popular culture has captured the industry's attention because, as yet, that's the road to quick and easy profits. But these other, larger segments of the population are ready and eager to be served.

As the paradigm of interdependence and love replaces the paradigm of independence and fear, as traumas occur, perhaps even accelerate due to climate change, terrorism, and the compounding of global crises in the areas of health, economy, energy, environment, and poverty, the public will be looking for programming that matters—ideas, information, models, perspectives, and experiences that provide intellectual, psychological, emotional, lifestyle, and occupational advantages. Programming that enhances physical, mental, and spiritual well-being. Programming that contributes to meaning gives people hope for the future and empowers them to become more engaged in local affairs.

We got a taste of this in the weeks following the 9/11 disasters. There was an immediate and dramatic shift in the mentality and tone of television across the board. Suddenly, journalists and presenters were talking to us like adults, referencing at once our vulnerability and interconnectedness, the strength of the ties that bind and define us as a people. It was a demonstration of *real value* television. What we got from it transcended news and information. It was mindful, even soulful at times. It facilitated our connection in a variety of ways, and united us. Learning accelerated. And we were talking together rather than at odds with one another. With few exceptions, competition, everyday prejudices, glamour and gossip, even political differences became unsuitable topics for television. The industry stepped up and displayed its more mature potentials. And the public took notice.

While the strategy of *broad*-casting, maximizing viewers for advertisers, is likely to continue, *narrow*-casting has far greater potential for sustainability. For proof of this we need only look to the social networks where overnight, information, images, and video clips go viral because they appeal to special interest communities.

Structurally, the reliance upon established, routinized, formulaic, and cost effective approaches to programming is a *maintenance* strategy, suitable for the short term but potentially disastrous for the long haul. Why? Because people—audiences—change. Their interests change. Their politics change. Paradigms change. The economy changes. Largely due to the personal computer and the consequent social networking phenomenon, learning is accelerating. People at all levels of society are getting smarter and making better, more deliberate choices. As a matter of economic necessity, more people are more involved in some form of education and personal growth. As a result, the social IQ is speeding up.

History has demonstrated time and again that the lasting enterprise is one that not only meets the current need, but also addresses those on the horizon. Audience demand is never static. It evolves. The recommendation for television writers, producers, program developers, and companies then, is to dedicate substantial time and attention to identifying the direction of tomorrow's demand and gearing up for it. Dee Hock, former CEO of VISA Corporation, offers a hint:

"The organization of the future will be the embodiment of community, based on shared purpose calling to the higher aspirations of people."

Although advancements in the areas of television technology and delivery systems will continue to outpace our capacity to use the medium for enrichment and advancement, the direction of environmental, political, economic, and social change is likely to increase the pressure for more mindful, relevant, useful, and meaningful programming.

Admittedly, the programming under consideration here is not for everyone. Viewers or producers. But for creative professionals and students who are attracted to it, the following chapters provide guidance on how to make real-value programming entertaining, compelling, and profitable in many ways for those on both sides of the camera.

11

What Do Television Audiences Want?

Television should arouse our dreams, satisfy our hunger for beauty, take us on journeys, enable us to participate in events, present great drama and music, explore the sea and the sky and the woods and the hills. It should be our Lyceum, our Chautauqua, our Minsky's and our Camelot.

E.B. White

HAVING IDENTIFIED WAYS TO EXPAND EXISTING CAPACITIES and develop new ones, the next step is to understand how this kind of programming can be made entertaining or compelling, perhaps both. Actually, because we're talking about programming that matters *to viewers*, the challenge is not simply to invite or attract attention, it's to *demand* it by creating programs that viewers won't want to miss.

Of course this is not easy. There are no set formulas for success, not even in remakes of classical programs. No one can guarantee in advance that a song, movie, or television program will be a hit. And no one sets out to create a program that will fail. So with the caveat that program conceptualization and development are complex creative processes that involve a variety of skills and can take years of education and experience to develop, this section identifies some of the fundamental considerations of presentation, particularly those that would help writers and program developers create entertainment values for more mindful and meaningful, relevant and useful, real-value, socially responsible, subjects.

STIMULATION

Apart from diversion, relaxation, and keeping us company, the leading force that attracts us to our television screens is stimulation. Moving, colorful lights and sounds in a box. Understanding stimulation and using it skillfully is one of the keys to unlocking the door to viewer attention, enjoyment, and satisfaction, irrespective of content.

Stimulation is *biologically* positive (Bogart, 1966). When it's not discomforting or painful, we desire it. Television only activates two of our senses, so the experience tends to be passive. If the combination of sights and sounds fails to provide stimulation that causes us to think or feel, it can easily become boring, even put us to sleep. Psychologists refer to two types of stimulation: affective (emotional) and cognitive.

Affective Stimulation (Triggering emotion)

The challenge of television and film directors is to generate thought and/or emotion. They accomplish this through the skillful manipulation of the viewer's *attention*. The camera says, in effect, "Look here. Now look here. Now look over here..." Implicit in the viewer's sub-conscious is the question why: "Why are you showing me this? So what?" When these questions are asked and answered in the process of linear unfolding, there is satisfaction. Something is gained: knowledge, meaning, insight, or appreciation. And emotions are triggered.

All this happens because the brain-mind continuously makes associations between past and present experience: Is the current experience harmful and helpful? Pleasurable or painful? Good for me? Not good? If *association* is the mechanism, *empathy* is the energy that drives it. Together, these are the energies that pull us in, make us laugh and cry and want for more.

Association and Empathy: Association says, "This relates to that." *If I drive a powerful SUV, I will be powerful. If I dress sexy, I will be sexy.* If I do this I will get that. That's the mechanism. Empathy makes it work because it's the experience of standing in someone else's shoes, of *identifying* with another person's *interesting* or seemingly *desirable* way of being.

When we sit in the waiting room of the dentist's office and hear the sound of the drill, we get chills and try to shift our attention elsewhere so we don't identify too strongly with the unfortunate patient. Although we are not in the situation and don't feel pain, the sound alone is enough to trigger a memory of it. And we have an emotional response. (Sympathy is feeling *for* another, as when we say, "Oh, that poor woman." We feel sorry for her because bad things are happening to her).

Television and movies are empathetic media par excellence, not only because they combine sights and sounds to generate thoughts and feelings, but also because audiences want to *extend* and *deepen* the range of their knowing and feeling. Were that not true, love stories, and horror movies would have little or no appeal.

Thoughtful writers and producers take advantage of this mechanism by triggering associations with information and experiences already stored in the brain. Translated into a guideline for triggering affective stimulation: *audiences will experience the emotion that's depicted on the screen* as long as two conditions are met. Viewers must have similar experiences stored in their brains (this is why *universal* experiences are so effective. And the context, characters, and their responses to what's happening needs to be true to life. The stronger and more believable the association, the stronger will be the emotion.

So if one of the objectives of a program is to evoke feelings of joy, the technique is to depict *believable* joy on the screen and in a context similar to something the audience has already experienced. To increase the intensity of the emotional response, increase the intensity and authenticity of the screen character's experience. More association results in closer identification with the character(s) on the screen.

Cognitive Stimulation (Eliciting thought)

Knowledge is also biologically positive. Apart from being able to function in the world, the pursuit of happiness, meaning, and a comfortable life requires it. Knowledge reduces uncertainty and anxiety, satisfies curiosity, builds skills, bolsters self-confidence, improves relationships, and helps us adjust to change appropriately.

The challenge for writers and producers is to present information, ideas, and experiences (input) so viewer's make *cognitive associations*, connections between what they already know—or think they know, consciously and subconsciously—and what they have yet to learn. Particularly, viewers are concerned with the meaning and implications of the input. This too requires an

understanding of the target audience: their past experience, current knowledge base, beliefs, perceptions, and values relative to the subject matter.
As with affective stimulation, the tools of cognition—information, perception, logic, reasoning, symbols, models, and metaphors—must be true to life, ideally *justified* and backed up with evidence. Viewers expect the input to be accurate and true. And timely. If the views presented will oppose the existing views of the audience, a gradual and graceful approach will contribute to openness and consideration far better than an abrupt or aggressive one. Additionally, for cognitive approaches to be effective, the messenger must be credible.

The practical application is this: Know the target audience. And where possible, make positive associations by reinforcing or building upon what is already known or believed—as long as it's not inaccurate or untrue. When non-fiction television is boring, aside from production considerations, it's often because its creators failed to make believable, positive, even challenging associations between what they want to convey and what their audience already knows and believes.

APPROACHES TO TELEVISION STIMULATION

Appealing Subject Matter

The easiest way to stimulate viewers is to present subject matter which, because of the way the reptilian brain works, naturally attracts attention: human flesh and sexuality, violence, food, water, infants (especially the eyes), flowers, beautiful landscapes, furry animals or their representatives such as puppets or animated creatures. Of course, this is the mainstay of conventional television—and for good reason. It works! Use it. Programming that matters can be made entertaining and compelling simply by incorporating these naturally attractive subjects.

Communication Strategies

Another way to stimulate television viewers is through *communication strategies,* devices such as uncertainty, inconsistency, novelty, and change.

Create uncertainty by—

- Using a format that opens with a problem, challenge, or situation that calls for resolution

- Using sequencing that unveils only part of a process or technique, slowly, step-by-step
- Creating a context that generates questions and puts off the answers (resolution) as long as possible; the same with problems and solutions
- Creating a character who is stumbling, bungling, or failing in his pursuit
- Using counterpoint: The audio doesn't match the video; words don't match behavior; ideas clash

Create inconsistency by—
- Using non-verbal cues that are in conflict with what is being said
- Creating characters whose attitude or behavior contrasts with their values
- Having the actor or presenter express opposing or contradictory viewpoints
- Using a bait-and-switch tactic. Viewers expect X but Y happens instead
- Using humor that creates a reversal. "But seriously folks..." / "I lied"

Create novelty by—
- Presenting unusual or outrageous sights, sounds, music, or points of view
- Having a character behave or speak out of character; asides to the camera
- Presenting talent or performances that are unique
- Presenting unusual imagery
- Exaggerating differences

Create change through —
- Movement. If the talent doesn't move, move the camera; move both
- Editing. Change the camera point-of-view (POV); change the talent's POV
- Pacing. Use cuts and transitions appropriate to the sensibility of the content or action
- Use audio or music to signal a change in the story or content
- Content shifts. Make an abrupt shift from one subject to another, one emotion to another

12

Presentation Strategies

Anyone who tries to make a distinction between education and entertainment doesn't know the first thing about either.

Marshall McLuhan

HISTORICALLY, TELEVISION PRODUCERS HAD A HARD TIME justifying the production of mindful, meaningful, and useful programming to their superiors because it wasn't profitable. In the early days when regulation was fully engaged, "socially responsible" programming was just one of the hoops television stations had to jump through in order to have their licenses renewed.

Stations didn't resist because being seen as a good neighbor in the community had PR value. Independent production companies tended to avoid socially relevant programming, in part because survey results were very disappointing. And individual producers who relied upon grants or personal finances to produce this kind of programming had a hard time justifying the time, creativity, and money it takes to make it entertaining or compelling. Now, given the relatively low-cost of high quality production equipment and dramatically expanding and inexpensive opportunities for distribution, producers at every level have greater opportunity than ever before to incorporate high production values in their projects.

While the challenge of money has not and will never go away, the priority concern for both affiliated and independent producers is more a shift in thinking —from "People aren't interested," to "People are hungry for this kind of programming if it's well produced." (No talking heads please). It's a shift that can and does happen for producers who understand the packaging and presentational strategies that deliver both stimulation and real value. It's not only *what* a program says that makes a difference, it's *how* the producers say it. Substance and stimulation go hand-in-hand.

ABOVE ALL TELL STORIES

Story is a languaging structure, a method of organizing events, fictional or real, into a sequence—beginning, middle, end—that makes sense and reveals a theme or moral. The structure itself is appealing, compelling, and entertaining, because it taps into our survival and growth needs. It's in our genes.

From humanity's earliest beginnings, people sat around campfires sharing tales of the hunt and gossiping about neighbors. On up to the present, we lived and died for stories. Think about the stories told about the founders of the world religions. Wars are fought over conflicting stories or conflicting interpretations of the same story. Nations, cities, and corporations all have their roots in stories. Presidents and politicians are made, in large part because of their personal stories, the stories they tell, and the stories that are told about them.

Because stories largely determine what we consider to be real, the ones we hold dearest are those that connect us to the past, creation stories and the beginnings that gave rise to religions and nations, particularly our personal histories. Accordingly, these stories shape our deepest values.

In, through, and by the stories we hold in common we are connected to the members of our family, tribe, society, nation, species, and world. It's how values and the wisdom of the past are transmitted through generations. Ultimately, we are all part of one grand story, the unfolding "universe story" (Swimme and Berry, 1994). And now, the experts are saying that it's *television*, not the home or school, that tells most of the stories, most of the time, to most Americans. Particularly our children. For these reasons and because storytelling is intrinsically stimulating, it deserves first consideration as a way to incorporate entertainment values in television that matters. Stories, fiction and non-fiction, provide models for and evidence that the higher characteristics of human nature are alive and active in the world.

Although this is not the place to provide instruction on either storytelling or screenwriting, certain perspectives and techniques deserve highlighting because they are helpful in making mindful and meaningful content entertaining.

Story Characters And Presenters

The reporter, interviewer, or presenter should never be the story. As facilitators, they belong in the background. Make characters or presenters unique. Break the stereotypes. Make them real, vulnerable; flawed in some way. Assign them physical, psychological, emotional, and sociological characteristics. In spite of their weakness or bad behavior, the lead character must have at least one endearing quality. Some virtue. Otherwise we won't care what happens to him.

Make the lead character multidimensional. Give her soul, passion, interests, and commitments. Give her internal contradictions. For instance, the collector or builder of model airplanes who is afraid to fly. Identify one physical feature that would single her out in a crowd.

In fiction the writer must know the lead character's backstory. But don't *tell* it to us. *Show* us how it influences them. And don't reveal character all at once. Parse it out gradually. Let the viewer discover aspects of their character beneath surface appearances, through their choices and behaviors.

The lead character must be driven toward a self-determined goal, and the journey toward it must be difficult. She must fail along the way, and failure of the ultimate goals must have serious consequences. And make her motivation crystal clear. Why is she pursuing this goal?

Conflict is said to be the essence of story. Ideally, there will be conflict *within* the lead character as well as between characters. The more powerful the antagonist, the villain, the more glorious the hero's triumph.

A character's verbal and behavioral responses must be *believable*. Authentic. Prefer to convey emotions through action and behavior rather than words. We are what we do, not what we say. Skillful filmmakers and television producers show us emotion, they don't have the character or presenter tell what they are feeling. Documentary producers don't point a microphone in a victim's face and ask, "What was it like to be in a tornado?" They show the victim searching through the rubble of what used to be her home. Empathy kicks in when we can project ourselves into the situation.

And finally, show us the *consequences* of the character or presenter's journey. Somehow they must be changed as a result of their experience. If the story is one of personal transformation, show us the trials and tribulations, but do not neglect the triumph. That's the payoff that delivers satisfaction and hope. It's the characters and what they go through to survive or grow that drives empathy to resolution and satisfaction.

Story Setting

Take the audience somewhere interesting, beautiful, or unusual. Make the environment a character in the story, a place that makes a difference in the life of the character or presenter. A powerful way to do this is to parallel the physical or social atmosphere of the location with the emotion of the lead character. And use symbolism: rain as trauma or baptism; glaring streetlight shattering the character's preference for darkness; a fence as a kind of prison.

Story Drama

It isn't what happens that compels us, so much as *how* and *why* it happens and to what effect. Through speech and images, engage all five senses. Use visual language. Provide information by showing people in natural, believable situations and interactions. Set a tone and stick with it: Formal? Fast paced? Studied? Satirical? Intelligent? Sensual?

Don't *report* facts in a story. Instead, create a context or situation wherein the facts are revealed through action or interaction. As noted, show on the screen what you want the audience to feel. Make it authentic and real by seeing that all the actions and reactions are believable and justified. Leo Tolstoy said, "The best stories don't come from 'good vs. bad,' but from 'good vs. good.'" Protagonist and antagonist both have good intentions, just opposing ways of carrying them out. Conflicting "goods" can be even more compelling than conflicts between good and evil.

Story Structure

Beginning: Establish the character and setting—context—immediately and with action. Begin the story when a person or happening disrupts the status quo. Make the disruption or problem a universal human experience or concern, something that brings the lead character into conflict with the antagonist or opposing force. Have the strength of the villain or opposing force closely match the strength and courage of the protagonist. Here is where the protagonist determines to face the problem and she sets out to resolve it. Along the way, a key question—the "story question"—is planted in the viewer's mind. For television to matter, we need to know: Will she have the *courage* to face her problem? Will he *triumph* over insurmountable odds? Will she find *true* love? Will he make the ethical choice and live with the consequences? Will she *confront* her fear? Will he use his talent for *good*, or be content with fame? Can she *transform* her basic personality?

Middle: In the middle, things get complicated. Complication after complication, the story unfolds through a series of events. This is the plot. Complications must be happenings, not explanations. The lead character or presenter must care deeply about someone or something, or we won't care about him. Avoid speeches (more than five lines of dialogue). Avoid sermons and philosophizing. Crisis prompts the character to make a decision. Will he quit or go on? Will she take this path or that? Waves of complication after complication, failure after failure, lead the character to a final confrontation, the crisis that precipitates transformation.

End: The climax of the story occurs when the lead character has a transformational experience or insight in which he finds meaning. As a result the problem is solved. The conflict is resolved and the story question is answered. The life of the lead character returns to normal. He is content and moves on. Always, the ending must be satisfying with no loose ends—no unanswered questions.

Story Plot

Plot is said to be a character in a predicament. The lead character is on a quest to accomplish something important. The quest amounts to a chain of cause & effect happenings that are established, expanded, and eventually resolved. The character's driving force, the motivation that moves him forward through adversity must be rooted in a *strong desire*. Protagonists want something badly. And it's the pursuit of it that creates the complications. Things go wrong and they keep getting worse. The character's story *matters* to us, because in her frustrated desires and conflicts, we see ourselves.

A plot is entertaining when the goal is important, necessary, or urgent. Seeing it unfold creates viewer tension. So give the antagonist and protagonist conflicting but equally reasonable viewpoints. Heat up their conflict in situations where every action generates a reaction. And keep the audience asking questions, revealing the answers to earlier questions gradually. When the story question is resolved, quickly end the story.

COMMUNICATE THE CONTEXT

Another effective strategy for making programming that matters entertaining or compelling is to specify the context. This is particularly so for message oriented, non-fiction presentations, because the meaning of a message largely emerges from the context in which it occurs.

No message is sent or received in isolation. It's always part of a larger whole, an element in some ongoing process of understanding or perception, a fragment of something bigger or deeper. In order for a message to convey complete meaning, the receiver needs to know something about the sender, particularly their intention, motivation, and their desired outcome. Why are the producers showing or telling me this? What's the significance? What do *they* get out of telling me this? "Unless a message, whatever specific objective form it takes, is seen in context, it cannot convey meaning, or at least not the meaning which the sender of the message intended to transmit to the receiver (Kraft, 1983)."

In addition to being a carrier and clarifier of meaning, context influences content in ways that aid the brain's storage mechanism, improving information retrieval and recall (Hall, 1976). Context has been shown to be *essential* for learning and understanding (Flake, 1993). It's the natural means of helping the brain cope with information overload, and a necessary element of complete storytelling. It also improves our ability to read social signals, interpret our experience, assist others, and experience empathy (Hall, 1976).

"A student opened fire on his teachers and classmates..." That's a *headline*. Further elaboration of the details would constitute a *report*. Journalists may refer to the delivery of facts as "stories," but rigorously speaking they are not. They don't have a beginning, middle, and end. A *story* would establish the principle character(s), provide information about family, interests, or circumstances, give some background about circumstances leading up to the tragedy, tell about the incident itself and then the outcome. What was learned? How were people changed? Even if that information were available—which it almost never is soon after a tragic event—it would be too much to fit into a single newscast. It's not too much, however, and would be very appropriate for a single-story news program or special.

Documentaries, feature stories, and other formats can accommodate and benefit substantially by including contextual information. And they have the luxury of time to present it in true story format. The limitation, of course, is that complete information has to be available before it can be organized into the beginning-middle-end format.

Using the above example, consider a news program where an on-camera producer would say:

> *"Because this shooting in one of our schools must never again happen in our community, we thought it important that you should know the full story—what we learned about the shooter and his family, the victims, and their loved ones. This is a story, not just about bullying and alcohol, it's about good people ignoring the signs of a deeply disturbed young man, a story of friends not knowing what to do to help him. We'll turn to the professionals to try to understand how this young man saw himself and the trouble he had fitting in. We'll look at what provoked this incident. And we'll examine the school atmosphere, the environment in which this took place. Along the way we'll ask the questions you most want answered: Why did this happen? What should have happened to prevent it? How can I make sure this never happens to my child? And what can I do to become part of the solution? This is not just a story about the shooter and his victims. It's our story; the community's story. We can't do much about yesterday. But we can do a great deal about tomorrow."*

A more broadly contextualized story encompasses the narrower one, placing it within larger holons and patterns such as teen drinking, the breakdown of family life, failure to communicate, low self-esteem, the media's glamorization of sex, and violence as the quick and easy way to resolve conflict. Narrow or broadly framed, a contextualized story carries personal relevance: *Might this be happening to my kids?* And meaning: *I need to be more aware and attentive. When something looks suspicious, I need to respond in some way.*

Beyond making a program more relevant and compelling, context deserves a place in nonfiction programs because it builds *trust* between the producers and the audience. When we know where a company, producer or presenter is coming from—because the context makes their motivation explicit—viewers are in a much better position to evaluate the *text* (what is conveyed), the *subtext* (its underlying meaning), as well the *motivation* of the messenger. The frame alone communicates. It says the producers, distributors, and sponsors are confident in their presentation of the subject matter, and it says they genuinely care about the effect it will have on the audience.

Systemically, because human beings are interconnected and interdependent by virtue of their common humanity and sharing this planet, what happens to any one of us ripples consequences throughout the global body. When one person hijacks an airplane, all of us pay the price in privacy and restrictions. When one of us defrauds the health care system, the rest of us pay for it. But if we can't see the connection, if the relationships aren't made apparent in our television stories, we're likely to miss this fact and unwittingly allow the social body, eventually the civilization, to slip into bureaucratic congestion and eventually heart failure.

Philosopher and literary critic Umberto Eco observed that, "A democratic civilization will save itself only if it makes the language of the *image* into a stimulus for critical reflection, not an invitation for hypnosis." Clearly, what he said can relate to television.

If even partly through television we can come to realize that the stories of our lives are formative of the larger social stories including the species story and the universe story, then perhaps on the next turn of the spiral our children will be able to teach their children to respond to change in ways that are even more healthy, civil, and responsible.

SHOWCASE MODELS OF SUCCESS

Inspiration and empowerment can best be elicited by providing models of what works. In the presidential State of the Union addresses, consistently what brings both Republicans and Democrats to their feet are the stories about individuals who have overcoming obstacles. Other such venues where success stories are regularly told—and where cameras should bear witness—are plenary speeches at conventions, commencement addresses, awards banquets, corporate and nonprofit gatherings, and places where success is being celebrated.

Success stories provide evidence that difficult, complex, seemingly impossible circumstances can be overcome. Transcendence happens. And we need to see it. For one thing it gives us hope, but equally important is the fact that models of success can and tend to be replicated. Whatever one of us can do, others can do as well.

In the closing months of *The Oprah Winfrey Show*, scores of such examples were provided to show that television can and does change people's lives for the better. I speak from experience: My daughter volunteered in a Native American school for a year after graduating from college because of the community spirit she experienced on the television series, *Northern Exposure*. By showing us what's possible, models open the door to possibility.

SELECT A FRAME THAT'S COMPELLING OR ENTERTAINING

Studies show that one of the main reasons why, when channel-surfing, people stay with a program or move on is because of the format or genre. There's a long list to choose from, and they can be combined. Whatever the "picture" or message, choose a "frame" that will appeal to your target audience.

Actuality (live)	Fantasy	Newscast
Adventure	Game/Quiz show	News special
Awards show	Group Process	Performance
Biography	Historical	Profile
Comedy	How To...	"Reality" show
Crime	Infomercial	Romance
Demonstration	Instruction	Satire
Docudrama	Interactive	Science
Documentary	Interstitial	Situation Comedy
Educational	Magazine	Special
Ethnographic	Mini-doc	Superhero
Event Coverage	Mystery	Talk show

Formats / Genres

CHOOSE PRESENTERS CAREFULLY

On-camera presenters not only represent the subject matter, they embody the point-of-view of the program creators. Because their appearance and attitude combine to create a contextual energy field within which everything relating to the content happens, it's advisable to select them at the outset of a project, even build the program around them.

On television, *personality* is critically important. Viewers relate primarily to people, above subject matter, ideas, and information. It's why we anthropomorphize animals, why God has been depicted as an old man, and why college students make their course selections based on the teacher rather than the subject matter. An enthusiastic presenter can make even the most boring subject interesting. Conversely, a dull presenter can ruin a subject that fascinates us. Whatever the genre, the next time you're watching television notice how much of your interest or enjoyment is based on the personalities involved. Whatever the name we give to this attraction—charisma, chemistry, or rapport—personality is a key ingredient for making a program compelling or entertaining. Programming that matters requires presenters or characters who are appealing as well as knowledgeable and caring.

Besides the obvious qualities to look for in a presenter (professionalism, the ability to read and articulate spontaneously, integrate opposing perspectives respectfully, and maintain a positive attitude), the ideal presenter for real-value programming will be someone for whom the subject matter is a passion rather than a passing interest. They should have long personal experience with it. Much more can be learned from someone who has been on a quest or experienced first hand the fires of personal transformation or accomplishment.

MAKE THE PRESENTATION VISUALLY STIMULATING

Television is a *visual* medium. Avoid talking heads unless the context or format requires it. Even then, use it sparingly. Establish the presenter and the setting, then cut to pictures. And return periodically, briefly, to the person talking.

Prefer on-location venues over studio. Location communicates "real." Studio communicates "contrived." Use multiple cameras on-location to change the viewer's point of view (POV) and provide editing options. Single camera productions have the look and feel of news, whereas multiple cameras can simulate real-life situations where the POV is constantly changing. For this reason the preference in other-than-news situations is to avoid stand-ups and sit-down interviews. Although these can be very moving and informative, if the interviewee is not recognizable or if what they have to say is not compelling, use the interview situation mainly to gather the audio and edit it in post with B-roll to illustrate what was said.

The camera represents the eyes of the viewer. Its POV is their POV. In life, we don't stand still very long. And our attention moves according to the predominant stimuli in the environment. Especially movement. One camera can't do that very well. While it's looking at character A, character B's reaction will be lost. To shoot multiple takes of the action film-style, is to create a staged sensibility. Audiences can feel the difference. Of course, all options are open. The recommendation here is to make *conscious* choices based on clarity about which techniques best serve the combination of communication and presentation.

INCORPORATE SPONTANEITY

Spontaneous conversations and happenings appeal to television audiences because they are immediate and real, as opposed to being planned and canned. There's authenticity in observing the experience of other people's lives as they happen. We enjoy the unexpected, when things go wrong or turn out differently than the producer or presenter planned, especially when millions of people are presumed to be watching. It confirms that we're not alone in our stumbling and bungling, that our foibles and failures, wrong turns, embarrassments, and accidents are more typical than anomalous. And it makes us laugh.

USE EVERYDAY PEOPLE AND REAL-LIFE SITUATIONS

Stories and information about real people in real situations are poignant and compelling because audiences can relate to them. "There but for the grace of God go I." Compellingness is enhanced when the presenter or the screen characters are real people *experiencing* real-life situations. This is largely the appeal of "reality" programs. Their popularity is a testament to how much audiences want to empathize and experience vicariously.

The presence of a camera alters a situation. It can bring out the best or worst in those in front of the lens, so insure that the consequences for viewers are those you intend. Real life is where context can play a key role, as when the producers let the audience know how they came to the subject, why they chose it, what it means for them, and what they hoped to convey.

SPOTLIGHT PROBLEMS IN SEARCH OF SOLUTIONS

In one way or another, we're all working through personal, professional, and social challenges. While we don't want to get into a pattern of thinking of life as a series of problems to be solved, there's much to be gained from the experience of people who are either dealing with challenges similar to ours, or have dealt with them successfully. Television has made great progress in this area by providing tips and feature stories relating to personal appearance, health, relationship challenges, and home maintenance. But the field is much broader.

Health, well-being, and adjustment involve more than just our physical and emotional lives. We work. We learn. We interact. We have special interests. We have aspirations. We're on career paths and spiritual trajectories. We confront common frustrations when we travel, raise a child, move, search for a job, and start up business. The recommendation for producers is to tie the personal to the social, the higher level holons of business, community, nation, or environment. How does one woman's experience exemplify what's going on at these higher levels? And what are the implications and influences both ways? The greater the consequences for the greater number of people, the greater the compellingness of the presentation.

INCORPORATE NOVELTY AND THE UNEXPECTED

Novelty is one of the driving forces of evolution. Living systems are partly defined by their capacity to create it. Novelty gives them the flexibility needed for both adaptation and mutation. As old forms break down, new ones emerge from the field of experimentation, especially mistakes and failures. Because the brain-nervous system is so sensitive to change, novelty is an especially powerful stimulus on television. It's intrinsically compelling because unexpected or contrasting happenings stand out. They're recognized immediately.

The brain not only seeks novelty and surprise, it creates these experiences in order to enliven the present and prepare for the future. Far from being just another amusement or diversion device, studies show that novelty is a psychological need (Montagu, 1955). Surprise, the experience of the unexpected, is a cousin of novelty in that both derive from the same family of stimuli that distinguish foreground from background experience. Again, the senses are most sensitive to contrast—differences, especially those that make a difference.

We love it when top celebrities drop in unexpectedly on talk shows. Missed cues, out-of-sync sound effects, and presenters who flub their lines or fall out of character are compelling to watch. Novelty and the unexpected are among the main reasons why live, television prior to the advent of videotape was entertaining. Comedy is grounded in the unexpected.

So the recommendation for writers and producers of programming that matters is simply to look for ways to include elements of novelty and surprise, especially when one of the objectives is to entertain. When happenings or interactions on the screen are different than we expect, we're compelled to find out what happened, why it happened, and what will happen next.

USE TESTIMONIALS

Testimonials are insurance against making rash or bad choices. They are especially effective when the objective is to sell. When considering the acquisition of a new product or the adoption of an idea or plan, we seek advice and look to the experience of others in order to make a good decision for ourselves. We often choose movies, restaurants, vacation locations, and television programs based on what we've heard about them.

It's important to note that the strength of a testimonial derives from the *credibility* of the source. The more we respect the opinion of the person providing the testimony, the more likely we are to trust that the information is useful and good. Of what value is information when it comes from actors performing a script or playing a role, celebrities being paid to endorse a product, everyday people who are paid to give their opinion? What if these same people are *not* paid? Considerations such as these can make or break the realization of a producer's communication objectives.

MAKE THE PRESENTER OR CHARACTER MEMORABLE OR FAMILIAR

Paradoxically, television is compelling when it changes and when it stays the same. We crave change, but we also want familiarity. Getting to know television characters and personalities over time can be a joy. We count on them being themselves and being consistent. And when they are, we build an empathic relationship with them. We care about them. On the other hand, if there weren't some variation in their responses to changing circumstances, they would become predictable and boring. Characters who never learn or grow, who never falter or fail to change course are not believable. They can be exhausting to watch.

That we seek the familiar has been well documented in the social science literature. We read the works of authors we already like. We choose books, magazines, television programs, and radio stations within a narrow band of preferences. We associate with the people we know best, frequent the same restaurants, eat food in the same order, and take a longer route to a destination when a more direct one is known. There's security in the familiar. It can be trusted. We can depend on it. With respect to television, we return again and again to the same programs, characters, and theme songs. That's why several television manufacturers are putting "favorites" buttons on their remote controls. Programs we like are like old friends. They rarely disappoint.

For writers and program developers the opportunity is to select presenters or create characters with distinctive physical and personality features. Make their behaviors consistent, but over time put them in circumstances that change and challenge, affording them the opportunity to discover or express different aspects of themselves. As in real life, after doing battle with the forces of change, something of *intrinsic* value must be gained—a revelation or insight, renewed determination, hope for the future, resolve not to repeat a mistake, commitment to a goal. Something must be learned.

RESPECT THE VIEWER'S SENSIBILITIES

What would you think of me if I said in the introduction to this book that the information and ideas it contains are exclusively mine, that you're getting them first, and that you'll only find them here?

What would you think if, while you're reading this book on an electronic reader, I put a photograph of myself in the bottom corner of the screen and left it there, if I scrolled information about this topic across the bottom of your screen and inserted at the top a colorful graphic to show the television channels that are offering a lineup of mindful programming?

And what would you think of a broadcast network, affiliated station, or cable channel that displayed a small, transparent logo for only three seconds once every half hour, that never used the words "live," "breaking," "first," or "exclusive" in reference to its newscasts, that *never* superimposed *anything* over any program unless in emergency situations, that refrained from repetitive "teases," that consistently limited commercial interruptions to four minutes, and that ran only one PSA and promo every other break?

Enough said.

WORK WITH QUALITY PEOPLE

Finally, a strategic recommendation regarding the production *process*. Because a chain breaks at its weakest link, the challenge in putting together a creative team is to insure that every link in the chain is strong. Major production companies hire the best, most experienced people they can find. Successful producers and directors consistently engage the same people from project to project because, among other things, it reduces risk.

Program development and production are social activities. Whether it's working with another person on a spec script or a production crew, the quality of the outcome is significantly influenced by the quality of the individuals involved —their consciousness, character, creative potential, competence, and their ability to collaborate effectively.

Team-building is usually challenging. In many instances, particularly in corporate settings, the tendency is to hire the most experienced and competent among the applicant pool. Due to the nature of the kind of programming advocated here, in addition to experience and competence, the ideal candidate should also possess qualities of personality and character that position them for high performance, ideally synergistic interaction. These include:

Self-Confidence: Does this candidate know who she is, what she's doing with her life, and why? Is she her own person, or a people pleaser.

Socially Responsible: Does the candidate consider the consequences of his or her creative output relative not only to the employer and the audience, but also to the larger holons of community, region, environment, and nation?

Awareness: Is there someone home behind the eyes? Is the candidate awake to what's going on? Can she readily read people and situations?

Emotional Intelligence: Does the candidate have a temper? Is he able to identify, assess, and control his emotions? How does he respond in emotional situations? Has he any experience with conflict management?

Creative Intelligence: Does the candidate approach creative options as provisional, tempered by whether or not they contribute to the greater good? Because something creative *can* be done, doesn't mean it *should* be done. Creative endeavor needs to pass certain tests, social responsibility for example, before being approved for implementation.

Ethical: Has the candidate demonstrated ethical behavior? Has she given thought to ethical challenges that could arise in the context of the position she is applying for?

Open-minded: Does the candidate listen carefully and retain what he hears? Is he as eager to learn, as he is to demonstrate or teach?

Responsible: Has the candidate demonstrated that she's responsible? Can she be depended upon to do what she says she will do? Does she follow-through?

Positive: Does the candidate have a positive, "can do" attitude?

Professional: Can the candidate convey deeply held opinions, express emphasis or humor without resorting to coarse or vulgar language? Is his behavior and presentation respectful of self and others?

Quality oriented: Does she speak of "getting it done" or "getting it right." Does she perform as expected or does she strive to exceed expectations?

Higher motive: What drives this candidate? Paycheck? Perks? The work itself? Growth in the field? Career advancement? Making a positive difference?

Chemistry: Will the candidate fit well with the other members of the team? Will she respect them and will they respect her?

13

Communication Assessment Process

The more matter is organized, the more it is centered, the more conscious it is.

Pierre Teilhard de Chardin, S.J.

HAVING EXAMINED SOME OF THE COMMUNICATION TOOLS, techniques, and perspectives that contribute toward making a program compelling or entertaining, the next step is to build a solid foundation upon which to construct a program or series that will, in fact, matter. Recommended here as *essential* is a step-by-step creative process, undertaken with the goal in mind of producing a document that clarifies the concept.

Variously referred to as a *Project Description* or *Communication Needs Analysis*, the benefit of what I refer to as a *Project Communication Assessment* is that it precisely and succinctly identifies and specifies intention, which leads to the full development and elaboration of the concept. The process begins with the Concept Statement. Thinking it through and writing it down amounts to priming the creative pump, getting specific about what we *think* we want. Next, we pay close attention to every word, substituting or eliminating, distilling the original statement down to the most concise statement possible. Every word must be *accurate* and *necessary*. Only then do we address the next statement, the Purpose Statement, because purpose flows from concept. And so on through the document, each statement being perfected before moving on. In addition to developing creative projects, this process is very useful for developing any and all activities relating to one's personal as well as professional life.

CONCEPT

What is this program about? Write one paragraph that describes the concept, making sure that every word is accurate and true. If you're not clear about the concept, write what you know. This document not only *can* change, it *will* change. Use visual language as much as possible to describe what the audience will *see* and *experience*. This is not the place to provide information *about* the program or the audience. When you have a statement that works, go back and pay attention to each word. As you search for the best words, those that are accurate and true, eliminate as many as possible. The shorter the statement the better. When you're finished, distill the paragraph further into a single sentence. Separate it from the paragraph (usually above the paragraph, sometimes under the title of the project) and italicize it. That is your "log line," the briefest description of the concept. (The term derives from early Hollywood producers who kept their scripts in metal file drawers with only the spines showing. A one line description was taped across the black plastic spines so they could be read at a glance. Together in the drawer, they looked like logs).

PURPOSE

What is the program's purpose? What is its reason for being? Limit the statement to one or two sentences. Prioritize. What are the most important reasons why it should be produced? Specify its *communication* purpose, not personal or professional benefits. Pay close attention to the verbs.

If the Purpose Statement is focused and true, then the answers to the questions that flow from it will lead to its fulfillment. If the statement is unclear or scattered, work with it until it's accurate. If you proceed and decide on a different purpose later on, you'll need to go back and re-assess all the statements that derived from it, so take your time—days or weeks if necessary.

Examples of Purpose Statements that indicate the significance of the verbs

- The purpose of this program is to *provide* models of success…
- This program will *demonstrate* the many ways that people can…
- The purpose of this series is to *increase* awareness about...
- This documentary is intended *to spark* a national discussion on…
- As a pilot project, we intend to *motivate* potential investors…

AUDIENCE / OUTCOME

Who is the intended audience? Be specific. A shotgun approach such as "people," or "Americans" is not helpful. Examine the relationship between the project's purpose and its primary potential audience. If the relationship isn't yet clear, review the purpose statement to identify the audience that has the greatest interest in the subject matter or those most likely to fulfill the purpose. Once the target audience has been identified, it needs to be analyzed in order to understand its unique characteristics and needs, focusing at this point on those that can influence the program design.

Consider the specific group that has, or would have the most or vested interest in the topic. What segment of the audience would benefit most? In what ways?

A quick and easy approach to audience identification is to create a *persona* that describes in some detail a single hypothetical member of the target audience. Describe their lifestyle, purchasing preferences, and social circumstances. Include their television viewing habits and preferences, because that will be helpful further on. The following example illustrates how audience relates to purpose.

Purpose Statement

This public service announcement (PSA) will demonstrate the tragic results that can occur when driving under the influence of alcohol.

Persona

John is 22 years-old. He drives an older car. His first. He has a full time job, low self-esteem, and a girl friend he is trying to impress. He drinks beer because his friends do. Often. He is not a problem drinker, but a social drinker. For the first time he is in control of his life, enjoying the freedom of not living with his parents. He watches sports, comedy shows, and late night television. He's proud of his reputation as a "party animal."

COMMUNICATION OBJECTIVE

Given the purpose and the target audience, what do you want to say to them? If the program is nonfiction, what's the message? What do you want them to know or do? If it's a drama, what's the theme? When the program is over or the story ends, what should the audience take with them? An insight? Understanding? Knowledge? Appreciation? What should they know? What should they feel? (Refer to viewer outcomes in Chapter 8).

Confusion easily arises about the objective because there are often several desirable outcomes. The Communication Objective (CO) is about the *communication*, what is conveyed. It is not about the desirable outcomes for the writer, producer, or distributor. What is the program's message? What will it say? It's important to know this because, from a systems perspective, the program's content will flow from the CO.

If a program has multiple objectives they need to be prioritized. Most important first. A word of caution: because in the production phase time and resources are limited, each objective we add dilutes the quality and effectiveness of the higher priority objectives. If there are more than three communication objectives, consider multiple projects. Another reason for deciding upon only *one* or *two* communication objectives relates to the tendency for viewers to forget a program's message soon after experiencing it.

In the statements that follow, notice again how the verbs relate to *communication* rather than personal outcomes.

- In this series we will *teach* and *facilitate* three different meditation techniques: (a, b, and c).
- Viewers will *understand* the complexities involved in launching a new product line.
- This story is designed to *create* empathy for patients diagnosed with...
- These commercial spots will *cause* viewers to visit our web site.
- This pilot needs to *make* network executives laugh out loud.

PROGRAM DESCRIPTION

In order of presentation in the program, specify the content in three or four sentences generally. Beneath each description, elaborate the main points, features, or happenings to give the reader a clear picture of the whole program. If the concept is a drama, provide the protagonist's motivation and goal, identify the story question, outline the events that constitute the plot, and say how the story ends.

What if?

Concept

Each week a group of highly creative people—selected from local government, business, or the nonprofit sector—are charged with sitting together to imagine solutions to local civic or social problems which they previously identified. Weeks later they present a short video which they produced to illustrate their solution—as if the change they would like to see were already in place.

Subject Matter / Content

Live and on location, our host welcomes back the creative team introduced on a previous program. They tell why they chose their particular assignment and they talk briefly about the process of finding a solution that they could all agree upon. They show the video they produced and talk about the support and difficulties they experienced in producing it.

Viewers are invited to comment and offer suggestions and these are posted as graphics throughout the program. In addition, viewers are asked to vote "thumbs up or down" on whether or not they would like to see the solution implemented. If "thumbs up," the team is invited to make a formal presentation to decision-makers in a position to implement the solution.

The decision-makers could be the governor, mayor,, or other city officials, a corporate CEO, university president, business owner, or school principal. A new team and a fresh problem are introduced each week. The formal presentations air in follow-up segments. The participant's employers proudly sponsor the team members, providing them paid leave and resources.

FORMAT OR GENRE

Once the higher order components of the Communication Assessment have been addressed, a format or genre becomes fairly obvious. A strong format has consistency. The subject matter is tied to it in such a way that viewers return to the structure itself for a feeling of security. They sense the logic within the presentation as long as each program element relates in some way to the structure. Think of the program's format as the skeleton that supports and gives structure to the substantive content. In the example below, notice that the items described are those that repeat in every episode.

What If?

Format

"What If?" will be a weekly, half-hour, live, on location program dictated by the subject matter. The open will have rousing theme music. The live audience will consist of corporate employees. The on-camera host introduces the creative team and invites viewers to comment and vote. Viewer input is displayed graphically throughout the program. The team's video is shown. Following a brief discussion, viewers are asked to vote for or against the team's idea. The vote determines whether or not the idea becomes presented formally to local dignitaries. The program ends with a follow-up from a previous program to show video clips from the formal presentation.

PROGRAM ELEMENTS

Program "elements" are the technical and creative components that provide the vehicle for delivering the content. They combine to create its expression. These could include studio, sound stage, live-action, stunt performers, interviews, music, sound effects, narration (voice-over or on-camera), performance, B-roll, animation, graphics, special effects, presenters, actors, and other on-camera persons. These elements are specified in a list so readers, especially prospective producers and funders, can gain a quick sense of the project's scope.

PROGRAM DISTRIBUTION AND REACH

Where will the program be viewed? Where will the target audience connect with the program? National broadcast network? Local affiliated or independent station? Cable channel? PBS? Internet site? Corporate meetings or television center? International venues? Social network? When and how?

THE COMMUNICATIONS ASSESSMENT PACKAGE

Concept
The idea. What is this program or series about?

Purpose
What purpose will this program serve? Why produce it?

Audience / Outcome
Who is the target audience? What real value will they derive from it?

Communication Objective
What will this program communicate? What's the message?

Program Description
What will this program look like?

Format or Genre
How will the program be structured?

Program Elements
What are the technical and creative components?

Program Distribution and Reach
How and where will audiences encounter the program?

Part VII

Change

14

Transforming The Demand

Transformation is the process that facilitates the movement from limiting and constricting forms of identification to something larger, more inclusive, and more whole.

Ervin Laszlo

THERE'S NO QUESTION THAT THE TELEVISION INDUSTRY and its related hardware and software will grow and evolve. There is a question however, regarding content. Will there be real and regularly available alternatives for grown-ups as well as adolescents? Will television realize more of its potential to uplift, educate, inspire, engage, integrate, empower, and facilitate? Will there be programming that matters? Or will tomorrow's programming be more of the same? Given the industry's structure and financial success, is an upgrade in substantive, real-value programming even possible?

As consumers, the viewing public has more potential to effect *substantial* and *rapid* transformation in the area of programming than all those who own, manage, and operate the corporate networks, channels, and affiliated stations combined. This, because of the first commandment of business: providers must meet the demand. Also, it's in the nature of living systems: higher level (corporate) holons are constituted of lower order holons, *individuals* who think for themselves and make choices. The demand that you and I generate through our attention is the air that businesses need in order to survive.

Large scale systemic change occurs as a function of individual awareness and choice. It's the principle of "energy follows thought." Thoughts influence realities by directing our energy to the subject of our attention. What we think, see, desire, and expect, the sub-conscious tends to create. This is why prolonged, particularly emotionally charged, thoughts of "X" tend to attract "X" into our reality, whether or not we consciously want it. In systemic terms then, the challenge of transforming conventional television programming begins with changing how we think about it.

Danny Schechter (Television producer, filmmaker, media critic):

> "We have a technological revolution in this business (television); now we need a revolution of conscience and content."

AFFECTING CHANGE

Marketing professionals are watching and counting. Cable systems in particular know exactly, minute by minute, who is watching what. Advertisers, programmers, and producers use this information to insure that their companies are meeting the demand, maximizing their ability to target messages to specific segments of the viewing public. Every program we watch influences future programming decisions. From the point of view of producers, a program watched is a call to make more of the same. It's happening at the grocery store, in automobile dealerships and so on, wherever we make purchasing decisions.

Knowing that there are larger consequences to our viewing and purchasing choices and that these choices and transactions contribute to the shaping of a larger demand, we can make them with increased awareness and purposefulness —not watching programs that elicit negative thoughts or feelings, and deliberately choosing to watch programs that deliver real value.

Another way to change the nature of the demand is to provide feedback to providers and advertisers. This takes time and can be irritating, but television executives and managers, especially owners and marketing executives, pay close attention to serious comments presented in a respectful manner. Click on "Contact Us" at the bottom of the provider's or advertiser's home page. If you want a response, you're more likely to get one—and quickly—by posting your comments on one of the social network sites. Television enterprises actively scan these sites because a single harsh criticism can quickly go viral and have serious financial consequences for them. Another option is to search for and use one of the several dedicated web service that specialize in facilitating "consumer feedback" or "customer satisfaction."

By whatever method you choose, let the company know that you've adjusted your viewing choices. Say how and why. Suggesting alternatives is helpful. And it's always good to cite a model program in this regard. Most feedback tends to be critical, but it's equally important to express appreciation for programs that uplift or inspire. Now, because advertisers are shifting their focus toward a more diverse media mix, television executives are especially eager (I heard one executive say "panicking") to know what they can do to slow, reverse, or in some cases take advantage of this trend.

It's critically important to remember that *personal* transformation is at the heart of both industry and social transformation. The moment we make a good-faith effort to shift our intention, that is, choose programs that have positive rather than negative consequences in our lives, we have altered our course and kept emotional, psychological, and spiritual entropy at bay.

ACTS THAT DRIVE SYSTEM-WIDE TRANSFORMATION

- Dissatisfaction with the current reality
- Attraction to a more desirable reality
- Charismatic and frequent expression of a compelling vision
- Activation of will-power—deciding to live in the more desirable reality immediately, irrespective of how the herd is living
- Witnessing and sharing the benefits of the new reality with those who maintain the existing order
- Unifying events that bring together those who hunger for the new reality

15

Transforming The Workplace

Unless we put as much attention on the development of consciousness as on the development of material technology, we will simply extend the reach of our collective insanity.

Ken Wilber

THE TRANSFORMATION ADVOCATED HERE RELATES TO THE SHIFTS in thinking and their consequent practices as described in Chapter 4, specifically the "From" and "To" shifts in perspective. Essentially, it's an invitation for caring, intelligent, and creative people in and outside the television industry to consider a more socially responsible orientation to work and the workplace, one that invigorates and positions individuals and their companies for abundant and sustainable growth.

My disposition leans more toward evolutionary than revolutionary change, but considering the widening gap between the rich and poor—locally and globally—together with increasing changes in climate and ecosystems, a good case could be made for some urgency. In the area of programming, while I'm not arguing that real-value programming *replace* current fare, I very much would like to see it on the ascendency. And there are signs that it is.

SOCIALLY RESPONSIBLE BUSINESS

I believe the reason why the category of Socially Responsible Business is enjoying widespread adoption, is that caring consideration for the holons above and below a business has resulted in benefits well beyond but including financial gain.

These other benefits include increased brand recognition, product diversification, increased quality control, more engaged and responsive workforces, increased shareholder satisfaction, strengthening of the corporate culture, and more successful ad campaigns. The list goes on.

A company is considered "socially responsible" when its mission contributes to the common good. *All* stakeholders. This includes owners, managers, employees, stockholders, suppliers, customers, contractors, clients, consumers, and the communities and environments in which it does business. Its DNA, the soul of the company, is constituted of higher purpose, which is specified in its Governing Values package and executed top to bottom on a daily basis. In business parlance, its mission has "teeth" and "legs." And everyone has "skin in the game."

Even a quick search of the internet using key phrases such as *Socially Responsible Business, Corporate Transformation, Business Transformation, Organizational Development, Change Management*, and *Human Capital* will turn up many sites, including a listing of the current "Top 100" socially responsible corporations globally. Not surprisingly, many of the companies well established in this domain are located in Europe where social evolution has had more time to cook.

Because a television enterprise is a living system and all living systems are self-regulating by virtue of their being dependent upon individuals who make choices, it will realize its *optimal* success by *self-regulating* and by meeting the *authentic* and *higher* demands of its viewers.

One of the important roles of government is by imposing regulations to prevent businesses from harming individuals and environments. Without such regulation, businesses can and will do harm and justify it in the pursuit of ever increasing quarterly profits.

Regulation, the imposition of rules and the threat of negative consequences for noncompliance, can sap an industry's desire to take the high road of its own accord. Whatever the nature of the problem, outside regulation, although necessary, tend to establish a hierarchical relationship where one party is perceived as responsible, and the other as having license to do whatever is possible within the bounds of legality to make a profit.

Amazon.com
Anderson (Windows)
Apple Computer & Electronics
Ben & Jerry's (Ice Cream)
FedEx (Delivery)
Fender (Guitars)
Green Mountain Coffee
Honest Tea
Interface (Carpets)
Patagonia (Outdoor Clothing)
Proctor & Gamble (Consumer Products)
Seventh Generation (Cleaning Supplies)
Southwest Airlines
Starbucks (Coffee)
Stonyfield Farms (Dairy products)
The Body Shop (Personal Care)
Tom's (Shoes)
Zappos (Clothing & shoes)

A short list of socially responsible companies in the United States

Since the point of conflict inevitably revolves around money—irresponsible behaviors tend to generate fast and easy profits compared to responsible behaviors—business owners, managers, and even stockholders are encouraged to regard *money* as the sole definition of "profit." One of the characteristics of socially responsible companies is that they define profit more broadly, giving *people*—all stakeholders—the higher priority.

THE DEVELOPMENT OF HUMAN CAPITAL — EMPLOYEES

When employers *mandate* that employees conform to a certain way of doing things, or doing the "right" thing, it unwittingly provides incentive for *compliance* rather than excellence or innovation. Both parties become content to meet, rather than exceed expectations. Considering the law of conservation, that living systems tend to maximize the conservation of energy, this is understandable. Although there are exceptions and exceptional situations, we tend to expend the least amount of effort in doing what needs to be done.

In the modern age, the exchange of a person's time and energy for money has become the primary incentive for overcoming this tendency. Alternatively, many companies have found that productivity, quality, and innovation are best served when employees participate in the decision-making process rather than conform to the demands of supervisors. Besides taking ownership of the process, they experience the satisfaction and pride of having played a role in positive outcomes—the products produced or services provided.

This is especially the case when the employee's personal and professional growth needs and aspirations fit well with the purpose and mission of the company. When the higher good of the individual coincides with the good of the company, the definitions of "benefits" and "profits" expand and become more meaningful to both parties so that money becomes just one among many positive outcomes and measures of success. Beyond that, when a company empowers its employees to fully engage their heart's desire, self-motivation kicks in and performance greatly increases because the employee is no long holding down a "job" or building a "career." They're "working for higher purpose," according to Abraham Maslow, fulfilling their reason for being. Living what Barbara Marx Hubbard refers to as their "vocation of destiny."

Through the ages and across all cultural and religious traditions, people who have attained higher states of being convey the same message: The answers to life's important questions lie within. "Go within," they advise. Corporations and businesses have, with few exceptions, not heeded this advice. For one thing this *core resource*—variously referred to as higher self, soul, intuition, the voice within—is so deeply personal, people are reluctant to talk about it. Especially there isn't a context for it in the business world where the focus is exclusively on externals.

While church and home were the traditional venues for such discussions, the last few decades have brought technological breakthroughs in the field of neuroscience that are increasingly using scanning and feedback devices to explore the areas of brain-mind interaction, sleep and dreaming, psychic capabilities, meditation, and the whole range of consciousness studies, all of which are the domain of the interior life. As the ground of personal identity, perception, belief, expanded capacities, and motivation, businesses are beginning to see it as an important consideration. (Internet search: "Business soul.")

Norman Lear (Television writer and producer):

> "The next great improvement in the human condition will occur not through a millennial faith in technology but by uncovering a new, more spiritually satisfying notion of 'progress,' one that requires a vertical leap of faith, a leap in our inner development."

A growing number of researchers studying quantum physics and the fuller capacities of the mind are discussing the possibility that the *within* of both the universe and human beings derives from a field of "pure potential" (Laszlo, 2003). If that turns out to be the case, it gives *thought*, like stem cells, the capacity to give rise to form and make real the potentials we choose to activate. True or not the challenge to live comfortably within our skins and in harmony with the physical and social environment, is to listen to and heed the guidance that emanates from the core of our being.

Because that core, the defining and motivating source that generates purpose and meaning, significantly influences our decision-making and behavior, the ideal in the business world is not only to integrate the personal and professional, but also to continually insure that each enriches the other. I think of it as workplace symbiosis—mutually beneficial relationship and interaction, securing the success of the whole by attending to the parts.

Engaging in a process of mutual and continuous *inner* assessment amounts to respecting and empowering the employee's freedom of self-determination, while helping the company realize its purpose and mission. The place to begin is at the beginning of any major undertaking: engage the key players in a Governing Value Assessment (Chapter 6). When this has been done for the company as a whole and for each department, share the document with all the employees and *invite* (not require) them to use it as a model for conducting a personal assessment which they may or may not choose to share.

However it's done, the initial task is to communicate to employees that, because the company wants them to "live their best lives," fulfill their deepest goals and dreams—to the extent that this can be done in the workplace—they are invited to meet regularly with a mentor, perhaps an outsider or someone in the Human Resources department.

The mission of the mentors would be to create symbiosis between their mentees and the company. Their constant message: "You are an important asset to the company. As much as possible, the company wants to help you to identify and realize as much as your potential as you like, whether or not it directly benefits the company." The mentor then invites them to use the Governing Values Assessment process to identify their potentials and come back with suggestions.

Whether or not the company can help, just the knowledge that it has a genuine and continuing interest in helping the employee realize her potentials, establishes a more intimate and symbiotic relationship. What would the world be like if every employer presented this prospect to their employees? The reason this is so powerful is that it activates one of the fundamental urges of human existence, the unconscious drive within all of us that says: "Be more! And in the process, leave this world in a little better condition than you found it."

Establishing workplace symbiosis is an especially powerful beginning because it unites the individual and collective good. Whereas before the individual was the only one looking out for his becoming more of who he is, now there are eight, fifty-eight, or two-hundred and eight people who have a stake in him, including the contribution which he is now *significantly* more empowered to make.

This may sound impractical or unrealistic to some, but those who have flourished in such environments can testify to its effectiveness (Ardagh, 2005). When employees and managers alike collaborate from the *core of their being* on common goals, each contributing their unique creativity and competencies in a setting where the realization of their higher *personal* potentials and *professional* skills are encouraged and empowered, where their contributions are acknowledged, valued, and celebrated, *everyone* wins. Financial and other benefits cascade up and down the great chain of being. It's how ecosystems organize their parts in support of their purpose and function. The net result: the whole system thrives and evolves.

FOLLOW-THROUGH

When a company sends the message to its employees and candidates for employment that it's sincere about wanting to help them take their next growth steps, it needs to follow through. After the crucial process of assessing individual and corporate governing values, there needs to be a series of foundational meetings that result in a statement of policies and practices so everyone is clear about the process and implementation of regular follow-up discussions where each individual has the opportunity to express (as best they can and to the extent they feel comfortable) their personal and professional goals to a chosen mentor, someone who will work hard to create opportunities for symbiosis.

Periodic performance reviews are standard in many companies and institutions, informal in others. Recommended here and for the purpose of creating symbiosis, the discussions should include specific areas of consideration. For instance the mentor would ask the employee: What would you *prefer* to be doing that you are not doing now? If you were the CEO, what would you do to maximize your potential to advance the company's mission? Given your experience, interests, and skills, can you think of a contribution that you'd like to make on behalf of the company, the community, or our viewers—now or in the future? The mentor would also invite the employee to look into training, education, and other opportunities. And submit proposals. Employees with special skills or knowledge (related to work or not) could be invited to share them with staff members.

Whatever the approach, the goal is activating human potential. And it begins by acknowledging employees as a growing, intelligent, and creative assets, *partners* in the process of moving the company and its stakeholders forward.

Proof of the company's commitment to its employees in this way can be demonstrated by combining events that strengthen and unify the corporate culture with supplements to the employee benefits package. For instance, providing training classes and retreats, periodically bringing in inspirational speakers, facilitating small-group discussions, convening reading, research, and skill development groups, offering grants to attend in and out-of-house seminars and conferences, inviting "off-the-wall" ideas and project proposals, providing outside counseling and educational services, and mentoring in any area that contributes to self-definition, skill development, or group cohesion.

16

Nurturing Synergy

Synergy is the highest activity of life; it creates new untapped alternatives; it values and exploits the mental, emotional, and psychological differences between people.

Stephen Covey

IN SYSTEMIC TERMS, SYNERGY IS SAID TO OCCUR WHEN THE outcome of a team is greater than the sum of its members. It accomplishes goals that include but go beyond expectation. More needs to be said about it because synergistic teamwork, as Covey suggests, represents the pinnacle of performance in business and beyond. Practically speaking, synergy requires a *complimentary* circle of *equals*, individuals striving toward a *common goal*, working *collaboratively* in a process that provides each member *meaningful and creative challenges* which, when achieved, are *celebrated* together. The force that transforms a cooperating team into a synergistic one is *coherence*, which derives from a deep and shared caring and commitment to a goal or outcome. It's the *combined and focused caring* that makes the difference.

Something very powerful happens when minds and hearts are focused on a goal. Some call it love or passion. Others relate it to the law of attraction. One thing is certain: unified and focused caring insures attention to detail because each person owns the process and has a personal (as opposed to professional) interest and investment in the outcome. The characteristic signs of synergy include an eagerness to get out of bed in the morning so you can be with your friends, you're so in the flow that time stands still, you forget to eat and put off everything else because in comparison everything else seems trivial. You have peak experiences and intense feelings of loving what you're doing. Love of a vision and engagement in a process of realizing it can create strong personal bonds. When a team comes together like this, one plus one equals four.

We see it in sports and music, particularly in the military where teamwork can literally be a matter of life and death. Unfortunately, corporations adopted the term "synergy" in the eighties and turned it into a buzzword, sometimes the name of a company, to signify effective teamwork or high-performance. It certainly includes these, but it's more. An example is the high performance process "six-sigma," which has employees striving for zero defects within a system. Even there, the outcome is one plus one equals two. Rigorously speaking, synergy isn't about high-performance. It's about *transcendence*, overcoming individual limits and limited thinking. And it results in attainment beyond expectation. Having experienced it personally, I can attest that one plus one can equal four. Synergy is extremely delicate. It cannot be forced, but it can be nurtured. Even then, there's no guarantee that it will occur.

A MODEL OF SYNERGY (TRUE STORY)

In the context of a local broadcast affiliate, a producer named Oscar was charged with producing a series of thirteen half-hour children's programs called "Max B. Nimble." The context was a toy store where the owner, Max, playing a variety of colorful characters, interacted with children who came to the store with a parent.

The concept, informed by research studies, was to produce a series that would appeal to both parents and their kids so they would watch the programs together. Initially, Oscar consulted with and convened an advisory board of highly respected scholars and others who recommended story content and presentation features to insure the success of the concept. (It's significant that he attended to *audience consequences* first.) The lead talent, an actor whose real name was Max, had initiated the project and proposed it to the station manager. Next, Oscar needed a team. Having had an interest in psychology, he understood a bit about what it takes to create group cohesion.

He knew the positions he needed: writers, director, production coordinator, director of photography, editor, etc. Rather than assign people already employed by the station, he contacted individuals that he considered to be *the best* at what they did. He invited each of these individuals to lunch with him and Max without their knowing that they were being considered for a role. At the lunches he talked about the project and revealed that he was assembling a team of "the most competent and creative people" he knew. In doing this he established a foundation of respect. Also, by saying the creative challenge was so great that only the best could pull it off, he set the standard of excellence very high. So along with a salary, he offered each of the candidates a challenging opportunity to work with the best of the best. We all left our jobs and eagerly joined the team.

I remember feeling intimidated by the talented people that Oscar had assembled around the conference table for the first meeting. He handled the introductions personally. Brilliantly. Rather than have *us* give our names and tell our story, he introduced each person to the group by telling about our family situations, profiling our academic credentials and professional experiences, thoroughly embarrassing us by stating in glowing terms why we were chosen.

As I sat there listening, I began to realize what an honor it was to be included, and how wonderful it was going to be to work with such intelligent and talented people. After the introductions Oscar described his vision for the series, and introduced Roger, the head of the advisory board, who shared the research findings on children's television, acknowledged the brilliance of the design and concept, and said the series would constitute a grand experiment, possibly become a significant contribution in the history of children's programming.

It wasn't until many years later that I understood the brilliance of Oscar's approach. In that very first meeting, he established the *context* and environment for synergy to occur. Each member of the team was in love with the vision, eager for the challenge to play their part, and looking forward to the collaboration. The one thing that none of us, not even Oscar could have predicted, was whether or not there would be chemistry between us.

There was. Rather quickly, working relationships turned into friendships. The context again: We were delighted and privileged to be working with, "the best of the best." And we felt the pressure of living up to our reputations and the team's expectations. The process was exhilarating. Everyone worked at optimum creative output. We pushed ourselves. We wanted to. We had daily script readings and weekly gatherings of the entire group. Everyone was invited (but not required) to participate in any or all of the daily meetings, shoots, and casual discussions. It was all very spontaneous, relaxed, and fluid. We discussed every detail down to the batteries in the microphones and the sandbags that secured the flats.

I was eager to get to work to see what was happening. And at the end of the day we came together to talk about what had been accomplished, plan for the next day, and screen whatever was shot with applause and praise. Whenever something was going to be screened, Oscar put out a call for everyone to come and see. That kind of attention acknowledged that our contributions were both *important* and *appreciated.* It also provided feedback. The approval was intoxicating. The celebration of milestones, even the little ones, substantially contributed to our bonding. And although we didn't talk about it then, the coherence was palpable and we were realizing the vision.

We completed the thirteen programs on budget and on time. Management was so pleased they decided to syndicate the series nationally and they gave us a budget for another series of thirteen shows. And then another. *Max B. Nimble* aired nationally for several years, taking top honors in competitions, notably the Action For Children's Television (ACT) Award of Excellence. Parents enjoyed watching the program with their children. And the station received a stream of profits from advertising and syndication. Typical of synergetic interaction, the outcome of the two-year project was *significantly* greater than the sum of its parts. I think we exceeded even Oscar's expectations.

SUMMARY COMPONENTS OF SYNERGY

Complimentary Competencies

Members are chosen for their competency, creativity, and their fit within the team so their contribution will be *complimentary* with respect to the whole. An orchestra constituted of all violins will never perform a symphony. The leader must know which roles are essential and fill them with talents and abilities that compliment the others relative to the goal.

A Circle Of Equals

Synergy can only develop in social systems where the individuals involved regard themselves as peers. And this includes the leader, the person whose primary role and delight in the process is to keep everyone's eye on the prize. In practice this works best when this individual has the authority to structure the team. When a member is out of sync or wants to be the star player, the leader must be able to eliminate that member from the team. It's the phenomenon of "one bad apple." Competition, negativity, distrust, and star performance are all toxic to the nurturing of synergy. Team members must be equally competent.

A Shared And Compelling Goal

A laser is powerful because it's coherent; it aligns photons so they all flow in the same direction. This can occur in human groups, whatever the size, when the member's thoughts and actions are all aligned toward a common vision or goal with sustained focus. If one member of the team is ambivalent or wishy-washy about the goal, if he or she would rather be thinking about or doing something else, or doing it somewhere else with someone else, coherence suffers. Constituting a team that's committed to the same vision and eager to sustain their focused attention on it is hard work. It goes well beyond reaching consensus. That's why synergy is so rare and delicate. And that's why the leadership role—cohering the members of the team—is critically important.

Collaboration

Synergy demands that team members care more about achieving the outcome than becoming "star" performers. It requires leaving ego at the door and joining hearts, heads, and hands to make the outcome the best it can be. Effective collaboration requires that every member of the team feel respected and appreciated, and that their contribution matters.

Meaningful And Creative Challenge

Synergy requires that the members not only fall in love with the goal or vision, but also the work. It's easy to tell when this happens because people find that the word "work" doesn't describe what they are doing. "Play" is closer. The experience and outcome for a videographer shooting a commercial she doesn't care about will be very different for that person shooting a commercial that peaks her enthusiasm. We invest our intention and attention most potently in the things, processes, and people we care about. Essentially, synergy is about love.

Celebration

Celebration is a form of feedback. It informs the system and its members that past performance meets, perhaps exceeds, expectations. Celebrating successes and milestones, even minor ones, is not just a fun thing to do; it provides the encouragement that fuels tomorrow's endeavor. When we're part of a team and that team cheers us on, gives us a pat on the back, or a "well done!" the exhilaration encourages us to perform in like manner or even better. In truly synergistic environments, performance success trumps the paycheck. You can't buy love and validation.

Resonance

In whole-systems theory the term for personal chemistry is *resonance*. In the author's experience, it's an essential component of synergistic teams. Resonance involves vibration. At the personal level we speak of "vibes," the expression of a person's thought and personality. Their presentation.

Imagine a set of tuning forks set in a wooden platform, one for each note on the musical scale. If a separate "C-note" fork is sounded, the "C-note' fork on the platform will sound as well. Like triggers like. The frequencies are "attuned." By design, they are one and therefore resonant. All the other forks, those designed to vibrate at a different frequency, remain silent.

The same with people. We stimulate and attract others who resonate with our purpose and expression. We're said to be "on the same wavelength." Now imagine a work situation where a director and an editor are working together to edit a television program. If they're attuned—resonating—in consciousness and personality, they are likely to work well together. If not, not so much, no matter the context, circumstances, or compensation. Without resonance, coherence is unlikely. Certainly, they can get the job done and done well. But it's a situation where one plus one equals two.

Part VIII

Getting Started

17

Opportunities, Strategies and Industry Protocols

A new generation now has the chance to put the vision back into television and to travel from the wasteland to the promised land.

Newton Minnow

IF YOU HAVE $80M - $100M

Would you like to—

- Significantly and relatively quickly raise the educational and awareness level of the general population?
- Facilitate improvement of the human condition and activate human potential by providing models of higher human characteristics on television?
- Activate some of the higher capacities of television?
- See television used as a catalyst to inspire and empower people to serve others and the world?
- Expose the masses to the knowledge, expertise, and wisdom of the great minds and souls of our time?
- Provide television industries around the world with a model of socially responsible, real-value programming?
- Display on television the power of the combined forces of love, cooperation, and diversity?
- Stimulate and empower the political will to develop innovations in energy, environment, and community development?
- Make a grand and lasting contribution to human development globally?

If so, consider the prospect of creating a combined television and internet service that would be grounded in the new paradigm and the principles of whole-systems theory, a channel that functions as a responsible social nervous system, offering a full schedule of programming that matters.

What would that be like? Imagine a 24-hour, for-profit television and internet service that would inspire, uplift, and empower the realization of human potential by spotlighting, demonstrating, and celebrating the full spectrum of higher human characteristics. Having invested decades in researching, envisioning, and attempting to create such an enterprise, a good first step would be to contact the author.

IF YOU OWN OR OPERATE A TELEVISION NETWORK, STATION, OR PRODUCTION COMPANY

Consider the prospect of identifying and convening a core group of people in your organization to develop a vision of your highest ideals for television. With interest, the next step would be to specify that vision by collaborating on the development of a Governing Values Package.

Give the project a title that pops. Create a short and exciting promotional video to get buy-in from others in the organization. Plant a seed and let it grow. Spread the word and invite experts in the areas of content and presentation to the table to discuss possibilities. Convene small groups and ask them on an exploratory, voluntary basis to envision a new, transformed company structure or programming schedule—whatever is being considered.

With the benefit of the specifics gained, move into the research and development phase. Experiment with new programming concepts. Produce a pilot project and test it to see if the entertainment and production values are delivering the content adequately and appropriately. Share the results with all stakeholders. Then produce a top-quality video that comprehensively describes and establishes the new direction. Nurture the seed. See what it wants to become.

IF YOU ARE EMPLOYED IN A COMPANY THAT HAS PRODUCTION FACILITIES

Consider the prospect of identifying and convening a group of employees you think might share the vision of what you would like to do. A good way to initiate is to write a one page statement of intention and send it to prospects. Those who resonate with your intention will show up.

Articulate the vision and invite collaboration on refining it. (Do not invite feedback or criticism at this point because it could dampen your enthusiasm.) With interest, work on the vision or concept until it satisfies the core group. Develop a *small* and *doable* pilot project given the resources at hand. Consider the ethics very carefully: Would it be appropriate (or not) for the group to use the company's facilities and equipment for such a project? Can it (or should it not) be done on company time? Should other employees be invited to participate? Who needs to know? What permissions will be needed? If the decision is *not* to involve the company or supervisors, then the gatherings should be held elsewhere and the work should continue in compliance with company policy and without any conflicts of interest.

The strategy here is for a small group of creative and committed individuals to come together to design and produce a pilot program that can be used to leverage the next step—a concept or program intended for sale.

IF YOU WOULD LIKE TO CREATE A SMALL PROGRAM DEVELOPMENT OR PRODUCTION COMPANY

Consider starting a business positioned to offer services such as script writing, concept or program development, or video production. The market for these in the area of drama productions is largely, some would say "exclusively" in Los Angeles. Nonfiction programming can be produced and sold in any of the major television markets.

Twelve steps and a little advice—

1. Research how to start up a small business. Talk to people who have done something similar.
2. Create a Governing Values Package and then a Business Plan.
3. Produce a demo of your product or services so you have something tangible to present. Do not skip this step! It's essential.
4. Begin simply. No overhead. Work with the best people possible. Resist the temptation to purchase equipment. It'll be obsolete in three years.
5. Create promotional materials: business cards and a one-page description of your product or service.

6. Determine your rate schedule. Contact established comparable firms in other cities to get their prices. Price your services a bit lower. Not much, however. Clients assume they get what they pay for.
7. Develop a prospect or client list. (Yellow Pages, internet, trade publications). Who regularly buys the product(s) or services you will be offering?
8. Make sales calls. Phone for an appointment. Always prefer *face-to-face* conversations. Prospective clients want to know what product/services you are offering and why they should buy from you. Experience? Knowledge? Creativity? What have you done to *demonstrate* that you bring these qualities to the table? To insure a callback, offer a day of your time or services at no charge in order to become better acquainted.
9. Identify an accountant who will set up and keep your books for tax purposes.
10. Consult a tax expert to understand the tax implications of your business.
11. As you do business, continuously improve your demo reel or other samples of your work.
12. Make sales calls part of your lifestyle. Without sales a business dies. If you want to spend most of your time *creating* rather than selling, hire a *trusted* professional to do the selling for you—full or part time depending on circumstances.

IF YOU ARE A BEGINNING OR ASPIRING SCREEN WRITER

Industry professionals generally agree: If you're serious about writing fiction for television or film, live in Los Angeles. That's where the resources are. And because that's also where the bulk of the business is, that's where you want to conduct your networking. If you write nonfiction scripts you can live anywhere, but you'll likely be doing business in the major media centers anyway: Los Angeles, San Francisco, Chicago, Toronto, New York, or Atlanta.

The process begins with a fresh or exciting concept. You pass it by a few friends. They think it's great and you're encouraged. Walk yourself through the components of the Program Communication Assessment (Chapter 13) to establish the foundation, the bones that give your concept structure. With the concept fleshed out, it can now be shared. Is it time to write a treatment or script? No. Don't invest time in writing without first addressing two essential areas: entertainment values and money.

First consideration: Is the concept compelling or entertaining as it stands? What about it will attract and hold the audience's attention? Rework the idea until there are at least two very good reasons why the piece will be interesting, moving, or enjoyable. Second consideration: Is the concept salable? As an extension of the Communications Assessment, specify the reasons why someone in the business—a celebrity, producer, production company, or investor would want to buy your treatment or script? Do some research to see how well similar concepts have fared financially. What makes your concept similar or different? What will give it value in the marketplace? (An example would be if the leading role were written for a major celebrity or movie star). If you have realistic and unbiased answers to these questions, give yourself the *green light* to go ahead and invest your time in writing the treatment or script.

If these lines of questioning turn out to be disappointing or fruitless, you may be wasting your time on a concept that sounds good but is not likely to go anywhere. Then again, maybe not. Writing for the learning experience or the shear joy of living in one's imagination for a time are equally good reasons, sometimes superior reasons, for writing. However, if you intend to build a career doing this and the intent is to sell, then the recommendation is to file the weak concepts away and ask the muses to inspire those with stronger sales potential. Follow the path of what works. When something is consistently not working, don't give up on it, but be open to more workable concepts. Sometimes the timing isn't right.

How To Get A Concept Into The Industry Pipeline

The Nonfiction Proposal

For nonfiction programs or series', the standard presentation is a 2-3 page *proposal* that introduces the concept. Describe the series. For instance, "*The Leading Edge* will be a weekly, 30-minute, prime time, on location compilation of feature stories that profile..." Briefly lead the reader through a pilot program. Indicate the host or talent. Ideally, share the idea with the talent and secure their interest before you make the presentation. Estimate the scale of production and its costs. When would the program or series air? Who would sponsors such a program? Why? Who would be the principals in charge of production?

<u>Presentation</u>

- Make an appointment to present your proposal *in person*. This is key! The television industry conducts business face-to-face, especially with unknowns, not over the phone, through email or the postal service. Establish a relationship and nurture it.

- Phone for an appointment. Introduce yourself to the secretary as a "writer-producer." Quickly specify that you are *not* looking for a job. Say you want to pitch an idea for a program or series. After you make your pitch, offer the executive three copies of your proposal, a business card and a DVD of your demo reel. Conclude the meeting by saying you will call to follow up. Doing so demonstrates that you are responsible.
- If you want to stand out from the competition, send a *handwritten* thank-you note immediately after the meeting.
- Three days later phone the executive and ask if he or she has any questions regarding the proposal. Build the relationship by finding any excuse you can to meet face-to-face as often as possible. Managers do business with people they know and trust.

The Drama Outline or Treatment

The standard for the initial presentation of *fiction* is a treatment, a condensed version of the proposed movie or television program. Typically a treatment is 8 to 10 pages. In some instances they can go as high as one page for every script page—120 pages for a feature-length dramatic production depending on the scale of the project. Treatments are generally submitted to celebrities, movie stars, producers, investors, or development executives who make purchasing decisions on behalf of studios, production companies, television and cable networks.

Although the purpose of a drama treatment is to sell the concept, they are sometimes sold as products in themselves. For instance, a studio or production company will *purchase* or *option* a treatment in order to have the first right to produce it (thereby blocking the rights of others), so they can buy some time to work our details, attempt to secure an all-star cast, postpone the production decision, or complete projects already on the table.

Presentation

Identify the individuals and companies that purchase scripts. Companies that will review materials often have their guidelines for submission on-line. Those that say they will not consider unsolicited materials find their programming ideas through personal recommendations. Otherwise, ascertain the name of the individual (by phone or email) who makes purchasing decisions. Contact them to determine what kinds of stories interest them and if they would consider your program concept—which you convey very briefly.

The typical presentation consists of a query letter and a copy of the treatment or spec-script (a script written without any prior guarantee that it would be purchased. The writer *speculates* that the script will be purchased. Most scripts are speculative). Mail what you have along with a business card and a cover-letter in which you say you will call in two weeks to check the status.

IF YOU ARE A COLLEGE STUDENT ASPIRING TO WRITE OR PRODUCE REAL-VALUE PROGRAMMING

Choose your *teachers* and *advisors* carefully. Whatever the course, choose professors who have both a *passion* for and *practical* experience with the subject matter. You want them to inspire and empower you to do your best work. Apart from production courses, subjects that contribute to concept development and expression include writing, speaking, interpersonal communication, rhetoric, drama, psychology and the humanities, especially philosophy and history.

Truth be told, media employers don't much care what undergraduate school you attended, what courses you took, or your grades—unless you graduate with honors. What they pay a great deal of attention to is your ability to articulate, your personal presentation, the skills you bring to the table, and your character, all of which is evidenced by letters of recommendation from teachers and former employers. The person you are working for today is the one who can be of the most help in getting you situated in what you want to do tomorrow—by writing you a glowing letter of recommendation. So make every teacher and employer with whom you resonate, a friend. And stay in touch. The rungs on the ladder of advancement are *people*. Not just good works.

In and outside the class context, write as much as you can. Pretend that you're writing for a future employer as much as to meet your course requirements. The same with production classes. Produce as much as you can and approach each assignment as if it will be a standout piece for your demo reel. If your class assignments aren't challenging or wouldn't represent your special interest or ability very well, create self-assignments that will. Self-assignments demonstrate self-motivation and focus to prospective employers.

Prefer several small productions rather than a big one. The temptation is to produce *Gone With The Wind*, or a documentary on legalizing recreational drugs. Resist it. Demo reels contain clips that are usually no longer than a minute. So go for variety and uniqueness to demonstrate your creativity and skills.

If you're reading this it's likely that you're attracted to the idea and benefits of creating real-value programming. You could then, approach each of your class assignments as if they are opportunities to work in this modality. Generate a Communication Assessment for each project. Write, produce, and direct news and feature stories, mini-documentaries, school promos, music videos, commercials, and public service announcements. Begin by deciding upon desirable viewer outcomes. Make the pieces mindful, meaningful, uplifting, useful, or empowering. And experiment with techniques to make the presentation entertaining or compelling.

As you move toward graduation, ideally in your junior year, build a portfolio of writing samples. While you have access to production facilities and equipment —and student crew talent—edit together a 5-minute demo reel that demonstrates your ability to produce programming that matters. Many students don't find jobs in the industry because they fail to differentiate themselves. They say they can do it all. That's fine, but managers don't know where to place such a person. It's better to distinguish yourself. *Specialize*. Individuals who are focused are better at what they do and they're easier to place. Positioning yourself for a particular subject or skill track doesn't mean you're locked into it for the rest of your life. Not at all. It just helps potential employers to see where you would fit within their organization.

A former student of mine interviewed for a position as a journalist. She informed the news director that her specialty and "passion" (the magic word in business) was producing "upbeat stories, the positive things happening in the community." As part of her contract, she specified that she would not be assigned to tragic stories. They hired her and the news director stayed true to her request.

Get your work seen. Enter writing, film, or video contests, and festivals. Become involved in intercollegiate 24 or 36-hour production competitions. Upload your productions to the social networks. These and other opportunities to have your works seen are evidence of initiative and accomplishment.

One of the best things you can do to advance your career while you're in school is to take an internship with a company that produces programming. The more internships you can take the better. If only one, take it in the last semester or quarter of your senior year. It often happens that interns are hired after graduation. Choose wisely. There are more companies requesting interns than there are students seeking positions, so begin with your highest priority—the company that offers you the most exposure to what you most want to learn. Once in, do the job well. Exceed expectations. Especially, make friends with those in supervisory positions. Television is a *people* business. Managers want to hire people they already know and like. An internship is an excellent opportunity to demonstrate that you are competent, responsible, dependable, and likable: "Our kind of person."

After graduation

Jobs as such are generally *not* available. When positions open up, employers usually know the person they are going to hire as a replacement—someone they know and trust. New positions are rarely created. More often they are eliminated. When jobs in the industry are advertised in the trade magazines or on-line, companies become inundated with applications. That's the bad news.

The good news is that, because there's more work than companies can handle, much of the work has to be outsourced. *Contract, project* or *assignment* work is the first step toward a full-time position. (Try not to use word *freelancing*. It suggests you're marking time until something better comes along). When a position opens up, if you are well liked and you performed well on your assignments, you'll be invited to apply.

1. Prepare Your Presentation Materials

- Samples of your writing or a demo reel (DVD) no longer than 5 minutes. Introduce each clip with a graphic to indicate the role(s) you performed.
- A resume in standard format. The references you cite are critically important.
- Have business cards printed that contain your contact information and an indication of your focus.

2. Identify The Companies Or Organizations Who Could Use Your Services

- This could include video and film production companies, advertising agencies, corporate media centers, religious congregations, theater companies, and hospitals.
- Prioritize them into groups of three. Call the first three and arrange an appointment to speak to the Production Manager (or whomever would hire your services). Say, "I'm a recent graduate of (school). I'm *not* looking for a job. But I am looking for "assignment work" to help me determine my career path. I can (specify your skill set), but my *passion* is (specify)." Do not send anything through the mail unless requested. Your objective is a face-to-face meeting.

- In the initial meeting (which is not a job interview), provide the manager with your day rate. Make it slightly less than the rate you find from comparable companies on-line. Offer your first day at no charge, "So we can become better acquainted." Leave your materials and say you'll call in three days. Then call. Do this for three companies in one week. Two or three weeks later make appointments with the next three companies. And so on down your list.
- By offering a day free, you will be called. And that days work is your opportunity to prove yourself. If they like working with you, when a full-time position becomes available you will be invited to apply.
- The tendency in these situations is to look for what *you* can get out of these day jobs. Turn it around: The more you can do *for the manager*—ease his burden, have an enjoyable experience, make him look good, contribute to the bottom line—the more valuable you become. So even if the work they give you seems menial or boring, find ways to create value for the supervisor, the company, its clients or customers. When you are seen as a valued asset to the company, it's just a matter of time before you're in.

IF ALL YOU HAVE IS THE DESIRE TO CREATE PROGRAMMING THAT MATTERS

I learned the hard way that large scale projects are best begun by planting a seed and tending it. In this instance, that means identifying a programming concept that's representative of your desire and doable given the money and resources at hand.

As you move through the Communications Assessment process to define and focus the concept into a piece you want to produce, keep in mind four primary considerations that need to be aligned. *Consequences*. What do you want your audience to know or feel as a result of your piece? *Substance*. Above all, communicate! Deliver a message or create a feeling that delivers positive value to your audience. *Simplicity*. In the interest of clear communication, spend as little time and money a possible; the simpler the production and the shorter the piece, the better. *Quality*. Pack as much production and entertainment values into the piece as you can.

If you don't own a camera, borrow or rent one. Better yet, take the classes offered by your local cable access channel so you can learn production and editing techniques while using their equipment at no charge. That they will have the right to air what you produce is only a benefit.

The only thing necessary to purchase is editing software and a manual to go with it. Do whatever it takes to improve your production skills. College courses in production, lighting, and editing are highly recommended. Anyone can learn to operate a camera, but to *communicate* with one in ways that impact an audience requires an understanding of visual communication, its strategies, and developing "an eye."

The strategy of starting small is basically to create pieces or segments that both stand alone and can later be packaged into a whole program. For instance, a series of 10-minute profiles of the best high-school teachers in your area could be edited into an hour-long documentary or special that could be sold to a local television station. Generate the seeds, plant, and nurture them into trees. Over time, if you stick with it, you'll have the forest of your dreams.

Appendix

Original Programming Concepts

While the text provided examples to illustrate various aspects of programming that matters, additional examples are provided here to demonstrate the fuller range of subject matter and formats. Mainly, these ideas are intended to spark the reader's imagination. All of the titles are *working* titles, intended merely to suggest the subject matter or theme.

Although this book is copyright protected, the author freely offers the use or adaptation of the programming concepts it contains. Should they be used in some way, notification would be appreciated.

1. Cafe Dance

Frank inherited his father's cafe in Brooklyn. Maria was raised in Puerto Rico and was a dance instructor there. Together, they run Café Dance and are living examples of true love and a marriage that works. Every Saturday night they have an open party and give impromptu dance lessons in swing, tango, tap, salsa, ballroom, and country western. Because the music is great and the atmosphere exuberant, they attract the New York dance crowd. People come to watch, meet people, and have a rousing good time. Especially, they come to experience Frank and Maria who, through example and conversations salted with practical wisdom, help featured couples who are going through relationship crises. Frank and Maria talk openly about relationships. They may be blunt at times, but their example and zest for life endears them to all.

2. The Envelope Please

This series of special programs presents coverage of award banquets held by prestigious social, humanitarian, and business institutions. Beyond announcing the winners, the program consists of pre-produced profiles of the winners, highlighting the accomplishments that justified the award.

- Sara Lee Corporation's Frontrunner Award
- Avon's Women of Enterprise Awards
- National Wildlife Federation's Environmental Achievement Award
- Reebok International's Human Rights Award
- Amnesty International's awards
- Malcolm Baldridge National Quality Award
- Industrial Design Excellence Awards
- America's Corporate Conscience Awards
- Business Enterprise Awards

3. In The Spirit Of...

Sponsored, one-minute profiles of individuals or groups working in ways that dramatically illustrate a particular "spirit." A voice-over announcer introduces an individual or group that is profiled to show how they express and vitalize the particular spirit they exemplify. For example, Heather Kaplan, a 13-year old leukemia patient who created the Silver Lining Fund to supply toys and games to kids hospitalized with cancer, represents the spirit of *caring for others*.

4. The Greater Gift

This series focuses on the art of gift-giving. It's one of the most fundamental and important of human behaviors, an act loaded with meaning. What does is say when a child gives his mother a gift wrapped in a garbage bag? What does the obligatory gift say? How does it feel when everybody in the room receives a gift but you? What is the difference between a gift well wrapped and one merely wrapped? How do you know what someone would really like to receive? Why give a gift? And when? How do you receive a gift well? What sentiment or message do particular gifts convey?

The host of this program has the personality and passion to bring the subject to life. Segments deal with the purpose, meaning, contexts, protocols, timing, manners, and philosophies of gift-giving. And receiving. The program offers advice and practical tips through short humorous skits like *The Carol Burnett Show*, with a continuing mini-play similar in format to *The Honeymooners*.

5. The Explorers

This highly visual television magazine contains segments (like *60 Minutes*) that deepen our knowledge and appreciation of the planet. Segments include ecology, astronomy, biology, chemistry, and physics, presented to make connections between the knowledge and beauty of the natural world.

6. Body-Mind-Spirit

In this *interactive* hour a renowned trio of hosts, each having a specialty in one of the three areas, introduces an on location, pre-produced package and afterward invites a live audience to respond. The studio talk is interspersed with pre-produced profiles of people who've made the shift from dysfunction to balance, from anger to grace, depression to vitality. Allopathic and alternative approaches are equally represented. Tools and techniques are gathered from around the world. Basically, the series presents the leading edge issues and developments in the areas of body, mind, spirit, including their integration.

7. Kitchen Conversations

Opinion leaders invite friends and neighbors into their kitchens for spontaneous discussions on topics from the local and national headlines, mass and social media sources. Participants, selected by the host, are diverse, intelligent, well informed, articulate people, respectful of others who express opposing viewpoints. Each week a different host and location coast to coast.

8. Helping Hands

This live, weekly, local program profiles constructive community initiatives—large and small, individual and group, profit and nonprofit. Viewers are invited to participate. The purpose is to give the featured project or initiative a boost so it can take the next step in helping more people. Project directors tell their stories voice-over illustrative images. They talk about finances, volunteers, employees, consultants, materials, connections, and show the positive results of their work.

9. Day Light

This everyday morning show presents an array of conversation, demonstration, feature stories, interviews, and news pertaining to all aspects of personal growth, life enrichment, and social development. Each department is hosted by someone who has substantial knowledge and experience in their area. Before a live audience, they engage experts and others who present a topic, sometimes with supporting inserts, and then open the floor to questions and comments. Topics include parenting, nutrition, healthy relationships, self-esteem, spiritual growth, health, career advancement, and alternative therapies. A flexible format provides adequate time for each topic including discussion and "How to" demonstrations. It's the morning show not to be missed because it combines humor, meaning, inspiration, and useful information.

10. Earth From Space

One minute interstitials (brief segments between programs), perhaps used as the station's promos or IDs, featuring *live* images of the earth from space. Taken from NASA, Google Earth, or some other source, the segments begin wide and move increasingly to a single feature: From the Great Wall of China to rice fields; from the boot of Italy to the Vatican; from the jungle of Northern Guatemala to the ancient city of Tikal, from the Eastern seaboard to the Statue of Liberty. Music. No voice over. No logos or weather information. Descriptive words at the bottom of the screen, but only if necessary. Used as local station ID's, the last shot could pan from the TV station to a feature in the community.

11. Conflict Resolution

Experts in conflict resolution facilitate meetings between individuals who are in conflict: jocks and nerds, gays and straights, conservatives and liberals, corporate competitors, people of different faiths and ethnic groups. Before the program the hosts meet separately with the individuals in different rooms to get their stories and perspectives on the nature of the conflict. These sessions are taped. On another day, after the experts have viewed the tapes, they bring the guests back and both parties view the other party's video. Again, these sessions are recorded to get the responses they convey to the experts. The video from both sessions provides inserts for a weekly program where the guests are brought together face-to-face to participate in a facilitated dialogue. The purpose of the program is less about defusing the conflict, more about understanding the nature of and relationship between perception and prejudice including their consequences and the methods of conflict resolution. The strategy involves mining the stark truth, whatever it is. As perceptions and positions are clarified and the barriers to communication and understanding drop (and they generally do), the individuals are challenged to collaborate in the writing and production of a creative video on any topic they choose. These are then shown in the weeks to come as follow-ups. Corporate sponsors present awards & perks.

12. Mystical Paths

A personable and articulate professor of theology introduces the subject of mysticism and the guest host for each program. The hosts guide viewers into the heart of the mystical experience, illustrated by whatever visuals are available and supplemented with artwork. Although there may be ties to the major religious traditions—which would be treated—the emphasis is on individual experience, each program featuring the mystical experience of one individual. (If the person does not want to reveal his or her identity that would be respected.) At the end of the program the host provides explanations and addresses questions that naturally arise. Quotes from sacred literatures and other sources are superimposed where appropriate. The professor concludes each program with comments that situate mystical experiences in the context of science and society.

13. Nonprofit Profiles

This program profiles local and national nonprofit organizations *on location* so viewers can understand their mission, values, vision, and the results of their work. Without being sappy or sad, each program focuses on one organization, exposing viewers to the people—in the office and in the field—who are making a difference. The nonprofit sector plays a vital role in communities and in the nation, one that needs to be highlighted and assisted. Each is a holon that ripples positive energies above and below. The profiles include opportunities for involvement, but not appeals for support, although contact information is provided. The focus is the organization, what and how it contributes.

14. Indigenous Heritage

A Native-American host introduces tribal elders, storytellers, shaman, and everyday people who present their tribal histories and tell their personal stories. These in-depth profiles, illustrated by personal and historic photos, artwork, video and archival footage, convey the relatedness of the individual to their tribal traditions, and their connectedness to Mother Earth.

15. The Public Wisdom

A friendly host talks with diverse everyday people who have something to say or stories to tell and are willing to speak from the heart. These candid profiles focus on what people care about, what motivates them to do what they do, what they love to do, their unique talents, personal goals and vision, their faith and what they want for their families, communities, and world, including their significant, quirky, or humorous anecdotal experiences.

16. *Turning Points*

Each week a different celebrity introduces a scripted dramatic *reenactment* of a real-life event that turned someone's live around. As part of their quest to understand the theme of the program—personal transformation—the celebrity opens the show with a brief anecdote about his or her own turning point. On special occasions the celebrities reenact their own turning points.

17. Young Love

In each episode a nationally known film or drama celebrity directs high school and collage age students in the production of a mini play or skit that illustrates common relationship challenges for young people. After some instruction by their teachers, the students conduct research and write a script. Topics might include: When is intimacy appropriate? How to say, "No" yet keep a relationship alive. AIDS. Drugs. Fashion. Peer pressure. Self-esteem. Social networking traps. Mixed ethnic and same-sex relationships. Spotting disturbed peers and considerations of appropriate action. The involved students carry the program as cameras follow their preparations and interaction with the celebrity. The mini-drama or skit is performed and recorded in front of a large audience at the high school. The celebrity comments on the experience and presents gifts.

18. Building Our World

Each program profiles a well thought-out perspective, hypothetical or real, which contributes to positive *social* change. Hosted by a social engineer, the program introduces viewers to ideas and visions that rarely, if ever, reach the mainstream media. Positive social visions emerge in a wide variety of fields besides the social sciences: physics, commerce, transportation, communication, psychology, health, human potential, creativity, education, corporate transformation, ecology, engineering, architecture, nutrition, political science, space...

19. Education Magazine

This television magazine would be structured as a primary venue for a national conversation on education and learning. How do we learn? How do we learn best? What physical and social environments contribute to learning? What is important to learn? Departments explore the many and complex areas of education, taken in its broadest meaning as the learning process. Regular features profile learning programs that work, teacher excellence, and methods of bringing teachers, students, and parents together. One segment would profile the substance at educational conferences. Others would highlight Social and Emotional Learning (SEL) and its various initiatives, the results of learning research, opportunities for learners with special needs, handling violence in schools, learning disabilities and bullying.

20. Pearls Of Wisdom

These half-hour programs present *interpretive* readings selected from the great storehouse of human literature and philosophy and read by celebrities. Examples include Marcus Aurelius' "Meditations: The Stoic Ideal," Spinoza's "Ethics," Adam Smith's "Wealth Of Nations," Henry David Thoreau's "Escape To Freedom," Teilhard de Chardin's "Mass On The World." Done properly, they should elicit a "Wow!" response. Each piece could be sponsored. Put together thematically, they could be sold as videos. Promotional tee-shirts and other items with quotes on them could be sold.

21. Did You Know?

These one-minute voice-over spots, narrated by historians, scholars, or other knowledgeable people, present a snippet of local history. Some of these individuals can speak from memory. They convey anecdotes about neighbors and neighborhoods. What happened when—? What was the influence of expressways, train stations, inclines, trolley cars and airports? Fashion. Natural disasters. Prominent families and businesses. Entertainment venues. Significant events. All illustrated with vintage film footage, video, still photos, newspaper headlines.

22. Stats

Relevant and meaningful statistics are presented graphically in 10 seconds with related music. These selected statistics provide insight, promote understanding, or more accurate perception of the current state of the world, nations, communities, and the human condition. A ticking population clock shows the current birth and death rates by country. The number of people who read at least one book a year. How many people—in various countries—graduate from a 4-year college? The number of people engaged in scientific research. The total amount of federal income tax collected against the amount spent. The number and identification of species nearing or extinct in the last five years. The number of people in remission from various cancers in the previous year. Crime statistics by neighborhood, city, state, and nation.

23. Eco Update

One-minute spots that show what people are doing close to home to preserve and enhance their local environments. The results of research studies conducted by local universities. The initiatives and successes of local environmental groups. Homes and cars that model energy saving. Recycling. Research results. EPA, World Wildlife Fund, and other organizational initiatives. Tips for viewers who want to be part of the solution.

24. Nutrition Magazine

A panel of diverse and knowledgeable nutritionists interacts with a studio audience and viewers to discuss topics relating to nutrition. Departments include organic farming, cooking, chemistry, supplements, physiology, herbs, book reviews, and recent studies. Pre-produced on location stories examine farming techniques, rainforest remedies, juicing, irradiation, seafood safety, food combining, legal issues, cosmetics, suppliers, nutrition as a defense against particular illnesses. Someone from the audience is selected for a "nutrition and lifestyle analysis," the first step toward a health makeover. Graphics, animation, and a large screen video background provide additional visuals.

25. Personal Success

A renowned author and teacher on the subject of personal success visits with people from a wide variety of fields to get at the heart of defining success and what it takes to achieve it. These personal stories, illustrated with video footage and still photographs, describe the cognitive and affective skills involved in setting goals and reaching them.

26. The Business Of Leadership

Hosted by a business guru, this series of documentaries explores the many and various models of leadership in business. Cutting-edge leadership and management consultants describe their theories and strategies over footage that shows their recommendations in practice.

27. Wizards And Witches

A weekly, unscripted kids show where the host gives 5 to 9 year-olds conflict situations to act out and try to resolve. Topics include bullying, name-calling, talking to strangers, dialing 911, low self-esteem, lying, the Heimlich maneuver, television viewing, monsters, tantrums. The kids dress in costumes and act out what they think is the best way to deal with the conflicting situation. Overseeing them on green-screen so viewers see them as ghosts, are the voices of "witches" who prompt negative responses, and "wizards" who prompt positive responses. The conflicts rage until the actors get them resolved. Adults skilled in conflict resolution and child psychology write and provide the voices of both witches and wizards.

28. First Light / Night Light

First Light begins the day. *Night Light* ends it. These programs bookend the day by facilitating meditations and body-mind workouts. Experts and personable hosts, joined each day by studio guests (including children), guide viewers through a variety of exercises. Hosts are rotated every ten weeks to provide variety. *First Light* motivates people to get up early and begin their day mindfully. *Night Light* helps them wind down from the day in an atmosphere of calm reflection and appreciation. As a way to situate the individual within the larger context of life, the opening and closing for both programs would feature a *live* image of the earth from space.

29. Good day!

An *entertaining* morning conversation that features everything that's going right in the world. The male and female hosts of *Good Day!* engage in spontaneous and intelligent conversation, focusing on what's going right: achievements, social initiatives, creativity, community projects, people helping people, collaborations, and celebrations. This is not "nice" news, those human-interest stories about the dog that saved its owner from a house fire. These stories and issues relate to the higher characteristics of human nature, providing models that can be replicated. If the program makes the viewer feel good about life, work, and people it will have succeeded.

30. Good Business

A magazine program that features segments and stories about companies with a solid commitment to social and environmental responsibility. Background and history. Governing Values. Structure. Hiring policies. Benefit packages. Operations. The corporate culture. Social philosophy. Effect on costs, revenues, salaries, market share. Definition of success. How viewers can connect.

31. Synergy

Each week the host introduces a group that operates synergistically. The group is cohesive. They love what they do, and their output exceeds expectation. Cameras observe their meetings, celebrations, and working environments to show the dynamics of cohesion and how it is nurtured. Participants talk voice over about their experience. The host fills in the blanks so viewers can better understand and appreciate the psychologies involved. In some episodes the program takes viewers through an exercise as if they were attending a workshop on cohesion techniques: Rings of empowerment. Resonance. Rotating leadership. Envisioning. Positive feedback. Celebration.

32. The Eyes Have It

A highly respected and well-connected art expert (not an art critic) conducts on-location interviews that give visual artists the opportunity to show and discuss their work, particularly their perspectives on the creative process. Because the purpose of the series is to inspire and empower the creative potential in viewers, the focus is on the substance of creative expression rather than the business of art: style, design, composition, the aesthetic dimensions, imagination, sacred geometry, symbolism. The aesthetic quest and the creative process. Not the reputation of the artist or the art market.

33. Responsible Consumption

On location consumer advocates help viewers understand the products and services to avoid, where and how to get the best deals. Health and finance implications, environmental consequences, what works and what doesn't, scams, and opportunities. Viewers call-in. Email questions are answered. Segments include shopping tips, best prices, safety issues, improvements, product and service of the week based on customer satisfaction...

34. Neighborhood Tea

On location and in a different city and home each week, women come together to discuss their interests and challenges with the host of the program. Topics include balancing career and family, maintaining friendships after marriage and children, entrepreneurship, single mothers, same-sex parenting, health and beauty, managing money and time...

35. Matching Needs & Resources

Feature stories that connect those genuinely in need with those who can help. Notable individuals in the community such as politicians, athletes, media personalities, performers, corporate executives, university professors—assume the role of sponsor. They tell the story of an individual or family that they would like to help. Those in need are never shown and their real names are not used. The appeals are for food, job interviews, clothing, child-care, legal aid, transportation. The segments are posted on the TV station's web site so viewers and companies can meet the need at other times. The series is about helping where assistance is needed most.

36. Good News Headlines

A nightly newscast featuring the good news of the day. Good News is defined here as happenings that make us feel good about ourselves, our neighbors, or people generally, stories that provide models of what's working and people doing good works. These can also be incorporated in conventional newscasts.

37. News Dialogue

People who hold opposing views, values, or beliefs about a single current news story, come together *live* in the studio with a skilled facilitator to engage in *formal* dialogue. (Formal dialogue is honest, respectful, non-combative and noncompetitive, always holding truth-seeking and the integrity of the relationships as the highest priority). Apart from their direct involvement with the issue in question, guests are selected for their open-mindedness, ability to listen, willingness to be convinced, skill in logical argumentation, and the desire to champion harmony. Viewers are invited to "agree" or "disagree" with the points of view expressed. At the end of the program the audience indicates which viewpoints or arguments scored highest.

38. Rethinking The City

A small group of volunteers who want to face the challenge of improving their city come together under the sponsorship of the city planning commission (or some such group). Each program is produced in a different city. Using the facilities of their employer's (who might become sponsors), these people create a design and develop it into a presentation, perhaps a video, architectural drawing, foam-core model, or live performance. Their process is recorded on video. At the end of each program the host invites viewers to vote on the overall design and aspects of it. Prizes are awarded and the participants are offered opportunities to work on "real world" projects.

39. EO Base One

A science fiction drama situated aboard an alien spacecraft that travels between its temporary "Base One" that hovers beyond the far side of the moon and the Earth. The EO's mission is to prepare adolescent humans for appropriate, sustainable, high quality living for all, including responsible planetary stewardship in preparation for admittance into the galactic community of advanced civilizations.

The EO's only reveal their physical appearance to selected groups of children in various countries. The children try to explain the EO's mission and recommendations to their parents and officials, but the adults are afraid for their children. They try to find the ship but can't, so they think the children are imagining things—until the intelligence and wisdom they express revels otherwise. A grandfather of one of the youths believes them and supports them, but he lives in a nursing home and is confined to a wheelchair. At first he does not experience the aliens, but as he becomes more childlike, he does. His adult children think he's experiencing dementia.

In each episode the youths are invited aboard the EO craft to interact and converse with the aliens who appear to them as colorful, light-body, translucent humanoids. The EO's and the children examine and analyze real-world Earth situations (currently in the news) and practice simulations using images captured from television. They view projected images and holograms with sound.

The plots focus on relationship and conflict. Rather than provide answers to the inquisitive children, the EO's engage them in Socratic questioning which results in their increased understanding. For instance: the relationships between inner, invisible forces and outer manifestations, the difference between "power over" and "power with," the power of diversity, and how local neighborhoods can create cohesion and harmony. As the series progresses the kids go into situations in their communities where they subtly, sometimes profoundly, influence events so things go well. The story question: Will the adults wake up and realize that their kids have something important to say? The story conflict is between the kids who have higher knowledge and their parents who cannot or don't want to believe it.

40. Firsthand Reports

Rather than have news stories written and presented by secondary source professionals, this newscast features everyday people—educators, civil-servants, political strategists, businesspersons, police officers, and other professionals—presenting stories in which they played a principal role. Different from newscast to newscast, the information they provide is qualitatively better because it comes from primary sources.

41. Partners In Progress

A local television station forms a long-term, close relationship with a nonprofit organization in its community, and they align their missions to accomplish specific goals. Instead of having a particular program or series that deals with the area of concern occasionally, the station revolves its entire schedule—at least for a specified period of time—around the realization of their shared community improvement goals.

- The nonprofit organization provide leadership and expertise relating to the area of concern (the content), access to their human and informational resources, and personnel to insure that the journalists continuously get the information they needs to create programs.
- The television station establishes a situation room that becomes the station's hub of operations where a celebrity team of journalists serve the ringmaster function by introducing programs, departments, news, features, and commercial breaks in the context of realizing the station and nonprofit's shared goals.
- Writers, journalists, and producers in the situation room are mapping resources, charting progress along various lines, matching needs and resources, packaging feature stories, creating graphics, periodically informing viewers about what's being done and what they can do to become part of the solution.
- The station contributes a portion of revenues from advertising to the area of concern.
- Advertisers are acknowledged for the many creative ways they are finding to contribute to the stated goals.

The combined resources of the television station and its sponsors, which are now viewed by the public as socially responsible companies, enable the realization of the nonprofit's social development goals. The overall program uplifts the community spirit.

42. Community Call

In a spirit of fun, this half-hour program encourages and documents community involvement. City officials and the heads of nonprofit organizations, nursing homes, hospitals, police and fire departments, recreation centers, museums, universities, libraries, churches, assess and prioritize community needs, which they present to the program's several producers. Each producer takes a "need" beginning at the top of the priority list, and produces a program that conveys it to viewers. The producers serve also as the program hosts who invite viewers to participate in a variety of ways. The producer-hosts now assume the role of on-site facilitators who, in collaboration with the viewers who show up, take specific action to address the need. Their activities are recorded along with interviews. Activities could include simple things such as taking down political signs after an election campaign, cleaning up a river bank, or hauling away trash from an abandoned lot. They might repair broken walkways using materials provided by a hardware store (sponsor). More complex activities could include anything that the city or other organizations never get around to because of money or shortages of available labor. From the producer-host's perspective: "It's hard work but extraordinary leaders and citizens can get it done—and done right. Besides, it's great exercise and the pizza's are on us!"

43. Bridges

"Bridges" are very brief, pre-produced interstitials that create continuity while providing an enriching and aesthetic experience for viewers. Ranging from 30 to 60 second spots, these can be sponsored. Simpler is better.

Nature: Sights and sounds of the natural world. The nature montage at the end of CBS's *Sunday Morning* program is a good example. The deer in the forest, the dripping waterfall, the graceful swaying of sea grass, flowers in the meadow, raindrops on a frog pond.

City Beat: The spirit of the city. For example a dissolving montage of conversations with good-natured cab drivers, construction workers, waitresses, door attendants, bus drivers, tollbooth operators, sewer workers and waste collectors. Humorous billboards and misspelled signs. Tailgaters before a football game. Slow motion of a crowded street. Subway saxophone player. Neon signs reflected in rain-drenched street. Child in a stroller licking an ice cream cone.

Vision: A montage of diverse adults responding to questions: What is your hope for the community? If you were king of the world, what would you change? If you could have one skill or talent fully developed at the snap of a finger, what would it be? Why? How do you see God? How do you see yourself? What's the biggest laugh you ever had? What three minutes would you like to live over? What is the gift you are giving the world? What culture would you go back to and in what time period. Why? What would you want to see?

Bird's Eye View: Exquisite low-level aerial images of American landscapes, cityscapes, seascapes, deserts, mountains, plains, lakes, unusual geographic features, cities at night.

POV (Point of View): Everyday people in everyday situations give succinct answers to the perennial questions. Who are you? Who are we? What are we, as a species, doing here? Where are we going? What is worth doing? Instead of random, "Man-on-the-street" interviews or stand-ups, personable interviewers take the time to become acquainted with the people they are interviewing in order to elicit *authentic* and sincere, rather than *guarded* responses.

Workplace: Undirected images and sounds of people at work. With permission, cameras go into offices, schools, factories, and farms to oversee conversations and meetings showing diverse people at work, none of whom perform for the camera. True cinema verité style of shooting.

44. Masters Of Arts

A celebrity actor, different for every program, introduces a master in the fine or performing arts each week. The masters works with individual students, sometimes with a group, to take their work to the next level. What makes the program compelling is witnessing the master's passion, persistence, and spontaneous creativity as they press their students to bring out their best. The programs conclude with the students displaying or performing their work.

45. KTNV News—Facing The Line

This series of one hour dramas is set in a busy, big-city television newsroom. In each episode the lead characters find themselves facing ethical and moral situations that challenge them personally and professionally. The situations derive from real-world experiences in actual newsrooms and newspaper city rooms. Should an editor fire a consistently biased reporter when that person is the boss's daughter? What's the proper balance between journalism and entertainment in a newscast? When a subject threatens to commit suicide if a reporter airs a story incriminating them, should they air it? How much authority does or should the military establishment have over the news gathering process? Is it the reporter's duty to protect the public from information that might result in panic? What's should a news photographer do—aid an accident victim when no one else is around to help, or get the shot?

46. Great Speakers: High Noon

Every weekday at noon one of the great thinkers of our time gives a 20-minute, uninterrupted talk on a topic and at a location of their choice. These individuals come from around the world and include the full spectrum of occupations and vocations. What they have in common is that a diverse panel of esteemed scholars has identified them as being among the "greatest speakers of our time."

47. Take One

The editor of a leading journal on media ethics interviews guests and presents feature stories to understand the social challenges facing the news and entertainment media. Clips from movies and television combine to further illustrate the full spectrum of topics that come under the headings of media literacy, criticism, and ethics. Viewers are invited to call in comments and questions, and suggest future topics.

48. The Grays: In The Middle

In this psychologically complex, hour long drama Charlie Gray is an easy-going, laid-back, friendly guy. He's orderly to a fault and considered by friends to be reasonable, rational, and kind. At the same time, he criticizes those who don't see the world as he does. He feels alien in his middle-class world. His wife Mel on the other hand, is a free-spirited mess. She struggles to balance career and family, and a desire to make a difference in their community. Her best friend once referred to her as "a beautiful but emotional train-wreck." The Grays have two children. The son takes after his mother and the daughter is more like her father. In spite of their differences and the intense conflicts that ensue as a result of them, the relationship works. They find the middle way, the "gray areas"—where harmony is realized through respectful communication.

49. The Business of Business

This on location series of mini-dramas featuring well known actors, introduces viewers to the realities of the business world by showing the basic principles in operation in a wide variety of business contexts. The purpose is to provide high school and college-age viewers an understanding of business dynamics, protocols, processes, and etiquette to equip them with the communication and presentation skills they will need when they enter the workforce. The packaged series of programs would have substantial marketing potentials well beyond their air dates.

50. The Human Project

This program presents the local and national happenings of the day within a stated context—the advancement of the human project (which is not the title of the program). News stories and features are used to illustrate patterns in human development, including processes such as trial and error, learning curves, feedback, innovation, creativity, the survival instinct, social pressures, technological innovation, and exploration. Panels of social science experts—different for each program because of the subject matter—sit together and place the news stories within the broad social context. The series is intended to illuminate how events in the news are indicators of broader currents in social evolution so viewers can learn to do this for themselves. It's the passion of the personalities and the seriousness of the content that make this program work.

51. Fine Art Magazine

This television magazine becomes the national forum for the art world, providing news, feature stories, information, critics corner, artist profiles, demonstrations of materials and techniques, interviews, site visits, all relating to the fine arts. Calendar information is presented newscast style to inform viewers about gallery shows, conferences, workshops, and exhibitions. There would be many revenue-generating and cross-promotional benefits, including a bookstore department where books and art supplies could be sold. Books are reviewed. Artists and authors are profiled on location, and an on-air ticket office sells discounted tickets to museums and special events.

52. Cool!

An ongoing window into the consciousness and manifestation of popular culture to show how "cool" is being constructed and marketed. Young male and female hosts take cameras into the environments where pop culture is being researched, designed, promoted, and consumed. This includes retail stores, publishing houses, trendy restaurants, road tours, TV networks, recording studios, fashion shows, offices of clothing designers, and manufacturers. Rather than glamorizing pop culture, this program shows the hard work and creative demands behind the scenes, revealing that "cool," far from being an accident, is a well-planned and executed construct.

53. News Education

Many people are confused by television news. Business, legal, medical, and political jargon adds to the confusion. Following the nightly newscast, this brief segment features a team consisting of two journalist and two laypersons (different for each segment) who, in an inquisitive context that welcomes humor, engage in Socratic style Q&A to make sense of what was reported in the preceding newscast. Rather than commentary, this situation has the guests asking questions of the host journalists that viewers would like to ask. What were the events that precipitated a tragic incident? What can we do to prevent this from happening again? Is anyone addressing this problem? Who's responsible? What can we do? What do those numbers mean? What happens at an arraignment? How does bail work? How did the drug scene take hold here?

54. What The News Is Trying To Tell Us

We not only need to hear what's going on in the world and understand it, we need to *use* that information to learn from it. Personally and socially. A panel of knowledgeable professionals—psychologist, sociologist, medical doctor, politician, business executive—respond to questions put to them by a journalist. Questions derive from current local and national news stories. Why did this (tragic event) happen? Is this a trend? Why? What's the pattern? What does it mean? What can we learn from this? How can we prevent this from happening again? How should we take this? What are the implications? What would constitute an appropriate response?

55. Expanded Human Capacities

Presented in a *60 Minutes* format, journalists specializing in the sciences present stories in the fields of psychology, parapsychology, neuroscience, psi research, and physics in order to explore human experiences that are not well understood. The pre-produced segments treat subjects such as psychokinesis, clairvoyance, clairaudience, lucid dreaming, states of timelessness, mind-matter interaction, reincarnation, out-of-body and near-death experiences, spontaneous remission, and savant capacities. The stories focus on the research being done to understand the nature of these experiences and phenomena—serious scientific investigation.

56. Local / National / International Newscasts

Whereas conventional local newscasts focus on local stories and provide a smattering of national and international stories relative to their perceived significance, to distinguish itself from the pack and offer more than headlines, this television station has dedicated programs in each of these areas. Each has a distinct look with anchors and reporters who specialize in these respective areas. And because there is time, rather than present "readers"—a series of headlines—their stories provide greater depth. Images come from a variety of national and international "feeds."

57. Sky Watch
An astronomer host combines computer simulations, photos of planets, stars, comets, galaxies, and other celestial features of the *current* sky, with *live* images from observatories, satellites, the Hubble telescope, and the space station to provide the visuals, over which guest writers, poets, and other "appreciators" provide insight and inspiration. Music and appropriate readings from literature and cross-cultural space missions supplement to create an inspirational and informative experience. Rather than lessons in astronomy, this program—targeted to the general public—presents the beauty and grandeur of the cosmos.

58. Entrepreneurship
There's a right way and there are many wrong ways to start up a business that will endure. This series of programs, hosted by an individual who has successfully started up and sold businesses—and now teaches entrepreneurship—provides models of success, information and insight, everything it takes physically, mentally, emotionally, socially, financially, and spiritually to start up and establish a viable business. Segments walk viewers through the stages of concept development, business plan, team building, suppliers, financing, and establishing cash-flow. Along the way there are warnings about what *not* to do. Actual case studies demonstrate what works and what doesn't. With the right host and high production values, the series would have substantial ancillary marketing potential.

59. A Meeting Of Minds
Professors of philosophy along with leading authorities in the content area discuss the intellectual contributions of great thinkers. Video-recorded conversations and comments are edited into an A-roll. B-roll consisting of, illustrations, archival materials, movie clips, and computer animation of complex and abstract concepts combine to provide the visuals. Great thinkers could include: Albert Einstein (physics), Dr. Albert Sabin (polio vaccine), Henry Ford (manufacturer), Jane Goodall (primatologist & conservationist), E.O. Wilson (naturalist), Teilhard de Chardin (science and religion), Nikola Tesla (electricity), Mahatma Gandhi (nonviolence), Buckminster Fuller (social engineering), Carl Jung (psychology), Charles Darwin (biologist), Thomas Edison (inventor).

60. Dream Come True

A pre-produced program in which a celebrity performer invites an aspiring high school or college student (in their area of specialty) to participate with him or her in spontaneously creating a performance piece. Music, song, dance, rap, standup routine, dramatic skit. The program opens with a teacher informing the student that she has been selected by so-and-so celebrity to collaborate on a piece. After a flashback to the selection process, we see the first encounter between the student and the celebrity. Then comes their creative interaction, producing and polishing a piece that works. At the end of the program it's performed in front of a *live* audience in a special, meaningful venue. Should the piece become a commercial success, the proceeds go to the further education of the student.

61. Human Development Journal

Cameras follow a professor of human development as he or she visits scholars, scientists, authors, and others who have recently published in a related area: anthropology, psychology, sociology, market research, demographics, spirituality, body-mind research, education. The authors share the substance of their work and provide demonstrations with visual materials, some of it pre-produced. Creative production values and editing combine to produce a program about *ideas* that is both visual and compelling.

62. World News Digest

A compilation of the major news stories taken from the world's most respected news media. The model for this program is the *Utne Reader,* which publishes a compilation of the best current magazine articles. In this instance, it's the most significant news stories, gathered from the leading television networks around the world and aired intact, as they did originally.

63. Tough Issues and Possible Solutions

This program uses a single "hard" news story—in depth and in context—as a catalyst for a panel of experts to discuss the issue and entertain possible solutions. Because issues that challenge individuals and society can often be resolved by shifts in perception and their consequent shifts in behavior, viewers will gain insight into how they can most appropriately adjust their own perceptions. The process demonstrates that and how tough issues can be resolved. Hope replaces helplessness.

64. Bookstore

Experienced professionals from the publishing industry host a daily program on books and bookstores. They conduct interviews with authors, publishers, bookstore owners, literary agents, critics, and avid readers. Segments include on-location profiles and readings by authors. In the self-publishing segment, authors present their works and various companies explain their services for creating, publishing, and marketing their books. Through an interactive feature in partnership with a major distributor, viewers can purchase books at a discount directly from the on-air bookstore. The look and feel of the bookstore and its many departments (one for every genre) has the warmth of independent stores as opposed to the sterile sensibility of the shopping channels.

65. Effective Helping

Each program profiles a helping professional in the host's quest to understand the best means of being of genuine service to others. The featured professionals talk about their approach (voice-over) while we see them in the real-life situations they describe. The program is targeted to caregivers and volunteers, people who are or wanting to help others. Many people don't do so because they don't know how or what to do. Topics include giving and receiving, dealing with burnout, role entrapment, bureaucracy, touching, clash of wills, intervention, ethics, and mental exercise.

66. The Spiritual Quest

A magazine program hosted by individuals who have long and varied experience with the spiritual quest. Various departments provide contexts for the stories, information, experiences, news, and demonstrations, much of which is pre-produced. Although the subject of religion and its many traditions would be part of the conversations, the focus would be on spirituality and related matters, not organized religion.

67. Doc Block

Each week a different producer introduces his or her documentary. These could range from student productions on up to and including large budget productions. The documentaries are shown without commercial interruption and they are preceded by the producer talking about the production process.

68. First Encounter

Each program consists of a dramatic reenactment of a love story. Using unknown professional actors, these are the stories of how lovers first met and when they realized they were in a loving relationship. This could be love at first sight, pen pals or internet pals who never met, war buddies, people who turn out to be business partners, adoptive parents, doctor-patient relationships, life savers (heroes), and student-mentor relationships.

69. Envisioning America

This documentary asks diverse people across the country to articulate their vision for America. They respond to an interviewer's questions: What is your vision for America? Where are we going as a nation? Do you, like Dr. Marin Luther King, have a dream for America? What should be our nations highest priority in the next three years? For you, other than a birth certificate, what qualities define an American?

70. Occupational Profiles

A series of occupational profiles that provides young people exposure to a wide spectrum of job and career options. Psychologists in the area of early childhood development have observed that children can only do what is modeled for them. Typically, models relating to the world of work are few and narrow, provided mainly by family, friends, and the media. What's needed is a comprehensive series where a much fuller spectrum of jobs and careers are modeled, along with information relating to job descriptions, geography, lifestyle, qualifications, entry requirements, salary scale, benefits and liabilities, expectations and contextual structures. Produced with high production values and celebrity hosts, the series would enjoy tremendous opportunities for ancillary sales.

71. Parenting Magazine

A weekday morning program with departments based on the ages and stages of child development. The full range of topics are covered, not merely as quick segments or tips, but substantial information and in-depth coverage. Regular contributors to the live studio situation would include child and behavioral psychologists, early childhood development teachers, publishers of parenting magazines, and specialists such as neuroscientists, social and emotional learning (SEL) teachers and authors. The objective here is to create a forum where parents can connect with other parents and parenting experts.

References

Adler, R. P. *Understanding Television: Essays On Television As A Social And Cultural Force*. Westport, CT: Praeger Publishers, 1981.

Ardagh, Arjuna. *The Translucent Revolution: How People Just Like You Are Waking Up and Changing The World*. Novato, CA.: New World Library, 2005.

Barker, Joel. *Paradigms: The Business of Discovering The Future*. Burnsville, MN: Charthouse Learning Corporation, 1993.

Baskin, Ken. *Corporate DNA: Learning From Life*. Oxford, UK: Butterworth-Heinemann
Publishing, 1998.

Bateson, Gregory. *Mind And Nature: A Necessary Unity*. New York, NY: Bantam Books, 1988.

Batra, N.D.. *A Self-Renewing Society*. New York, NY: University Press of America, 1990.

Bennis, Warren. *On Becoming A Leader*. New York, NY: Perseus Books Group, 1989)

Bertalanffy, Ludwig Von. *General Systems Theory: Foundations, Development, Applications*. New York, NY: Westview Press, 1968.

Bogart, Leo. *Psychology in Media Strategy: Proceedings Of A Symposium Sponsored by the Media Research Committee of the American Marketing Association*. Chicago, IL.: American Marketing Association, 1966.

Buzzell, K. *The Children of Cyclops: The Influences of Television On The Developing Human Brain*. Fair Oaks, CA: The Association of Waldorf Schools of North America, 1998.

Capra, Fritjof. *TheWeb Of Life: A New Scientific Understanding Of Living Systems*. New York, NY: Anchor Books, 1996.

Dawkins, Richard. *The Selfish Gene*. Oxford, UK.: Oxford University Press, 1976.

Endemol USA. *Extreme Makeover: Home Edition*. New York, NY: ABC Television Network, 2006).

Elgin, Duane. *Awakening Earth: Exploring The Evolution Of Human Culture & Consciousness*. New York, NY.: William Morrow, 1993.

Flake, Carol. *Holistic Education: Principles, Perspectives and Practices*. Holistic Education Press, 1993)

Gerbner, George. *Television As Religion*. Media & Values, Volume 17, 1981. Reprinted as *Society's Storyteller: How Television Creates The Myths By Which We Live*. In the 15th Anniversary Issue, Fall 1992.

Gia-fu F., English, J. *Tao Te Ching*. New York, NY: Random House, 1972.

Greenleaf, Robert. *Servant Leadership: A Journey into the Nature of Legitimate Power & Greatness*. Mahwah, NJ.: Paulist Press, 2002.

Hall, Edward T. *Beyond Culture*. Garden City, NY.: Anchor Press / Doubleday, 1976.

Henderson, Hazel. *Building A Win-Win World: Life Beyond Global Economic Warfare*. San Francisco, CA.: Berrett-Koehler Publishers, Inc., 1996.

Hock, Dee. *Birth Of The Chaordic Age*. San Francisco, CA.: Berrett-Koehler Publishers, 1999.

Kraft, Wayne. *A Reason To Hope: A Synthesis of Teilhard de Chardin's Vision and Systems Thinking*. Salinas, CA.: Intersystems Publications, 1983.

Laszlo, Ervin. *The Connectivity Hypotheses: Foundations of an Integral Science of Quantum, Cosmos, Life, and Consciousness*. Albany, New York: State University of New York Press, 2003.

Miller, James. *Living Systems*. New York, NY.: McGraw-Hill Book Company, 1978.

Montagu, Ashley. *The Direction Of Human Development*. Princeton, NJ.: Harper & Bros., 1955.

Partridge, Donald and Lloyd D. Partridge. *Nervous System Actions and Interactions: Concepts in Neurophysiology*. Boston, MA.: Kluwer Academic Publishers, 2003.

Pearce, Joseph. C.. *Evolution's End: Claiming The Potential of Our Intelligence*. San Francisco, CA.: Harper-Collins Publishers, 1992.

Pirsig, Robert M.. *Zen And The Art Of Motorcycle Maintenance: An Inquiry Into Values*. New York, NY.: Harper Perennial, 1974.

Pert, Candice. *Molecules Of Emotion: The Science Behind Mind-Body Medicine*. New York, NY.: Simon & Schuster Inc., 1999.

Ray, Paul and Sherry Ruth Anderson. *The Cultural Creatives: How 50 Million People Are Changing The World*. New York, NY.: Harmony Books, 2000.

Sparks, Glenn. *Media Effects Research: A Basic Overview,* 3rd Edition. Boston, MA.: Wadsworth Cengage Learning, 2010.

Swimme, Brian and Thomas Berry. *The Universe Story: From the Primordial Flaring Forth to the Ecozoic Era--A Celebration of the Unfolding of the Cosmos*. New York, NY.: Harper-Collins, 1994.

U.S. Census Bureau, 2010.

Internet Resources

www.donedealpro.com

Everything you need to know before you venture into the business of scriptwriting.

www.productionhub.com

A practical resource for both screenwriting and production.

www.simplyscripts.com

Sample treatments and scripts. Status of deals. How to... (for screenwriters).

www.tvwritersvault.com

The television industry's project database used by leading Production Companies, Networks, and Agents seeking original TV show ideas and scripts for production in all genres of televised programming. Professional or aspiring writers and established producers may submit projects.

www.job-search-engine.com/keyword/television-program-development

This site provides a current list of positions available in the area of "program development." Includes internships and summer replacement positions.

www.transformationalmedia.com

This comprehensive guide to "life changing media," provides information and samples of what's happening in the areas of transformational and socially responsible films, television, videos, radio and audio.

www.tv.com/shows-in-development

Under the heading, "Forums" there's a long list of programs that are currently under development. Click on them to access a great deal of information about the project. These are especially useful for seeing how producers describe their concepts in one or two paragraphs.

www.soyouwanna.com/soyouwanna-pitch-tv-show

Provides excellent, very savvy, information about making a pitch. Also provides guidance on how to write a treatment.

www.noetic.org

A nonprofit organization that supports individual and collective transformation through consciousness research, educational outreach, and engaging a global learning community in the realization of human potential.

About The Author

David L. Smith is Emeritus professor of communication and former director of the Television Center at Xavier University in Cincinnati, Ohio. He managed the operation as a self-sustaining production company, created the production curriculum, taught dozens of courses including camerawork, directing, lighting, screenwriting, visual communication, and program development. His undergraduate degrees are in Broadcasting (University of Cincinnati) and Photography (Rochester Institute of Technology). His graduate degree in Communication with an emphasis in Anthropology is also from the University of Cincinnati.

As a scholar, speaker, and consultant Mr. Smith integrates a background in art, applied technology, and social anthropology in an ongoing quest to balance the traditional media with a more positive and socially responsible orientation. Mass Media and Broadcasting programs in universities in the United States and abroad have adopted his textbook, *Video Communication: Structuring Content for Maximum Program Effectiveness*.

Professionally, Mr. Smith worked in the industrial motion picture and broadcast industries, serving in the capacities of cinematographer, director of photography (DP), writer, editor, and producer of commercials, documentaries, corporate promotions, music videos, prime-time community development series', and children's programming. Before his appointment at Xavier University he was employed by Eastman Kodak Company, K&S Films Inc., Scripps-Howard Broadcasting (WCPO-TV), J&R Films, Taft Broadcasting Co. (WKRC-TV) and WNEO/WEAO (PBS) in Kent, Ohio. His awards include: Emmy, Cindy, American Corporate Video, American Film Institute.

<smithdl@cinci.rr.com>

Made in the USA
Charleston, SC
23 September 2011